Table of Contents

Introduction

One day at the company where I worked in San Francisco, we had a lunch party. Just for fun, we decided to put flags on a world map to represent where each of the company's 50 or so employees came from. We all looked at this map and saw that there was one isolated flag apart from all the others and thought it must represent an immigrant from some obscure island somewhere. Then we looked closer and saw that this "obscure island" was San Francisco.

The flag represented our one employee who was a native San Franciscan. This discovery resulted in a lot of laughter. We had employees from at least 10 different countries. We celebrated three different New Year's days: the international one on January 1, the Chinese one that has a different date each year, and the Laotian one on April 1.

You might want to try the world map experiment at your own company. You could be amazed at just how multicultural your workforce is.

Over the years, I have learned that working with and leading a multicultural company can be magical if done right. While leadership based on authority results in production—after all, people don't want to lose their jobs—what you get from leading that way is not a real team but rather a group of individuals with each doing the minimum work required to keep his or her job—not a truly satisfactory arrangement for anyone.

I eventually worked out a formula for success in leading a multicultural workforce that resulted in a team of motivated people who worked together while retaining their individuality. I call my formula F.U.N. management: F for fun, U for unique, and N for nurturing. I've seen this management approach break down cultural and language barriers while enabling leaders to get the maximum contribution from a workforce made up of people from varied cultural backgrounds.

One of the people I learned from was my former assistant, Steve, from Hong Kong. Just by being himself, Steve demonstrated a great example of how to successfully lead in a multicultural environment. Steve loved to cook, and whenever we had a company party—we had many parties at this company, including celebrating meeting monthly production goals, as well as traditional holidays—Steve voluntarily went to the market on his own time to buy fresh fish or oysters that he cooked himself.

I noticed how Steve repeatedly encouraged everyone to meet the production goal by getting them to think about why it was important: that it was good not only for the company but also for all of us. I saw how he didn't just talk but set a great example. He worked hard, and so did everyone else—to meet production goals and to earn his curried chicken, sautéed crab dishes, barbecues, and other scrumptious rewards.

Steve played a big part in the company's astonishing success, which over time grew from $4 million to $10 million and beyond. The individuals in the company worked together like members of a family.

Steve taught me a great deal about leadership and how a great leader doesn't always have to appear to be leading. I learned that when you work with a multicultural workforce, it's essential to communicate with and understand each individual and their needs. You also must set the right goals (high but not impossible to reach) and make achieving those goals a team activity, with each individual understanding the goals' importance and contributing all they can because they *want* to.

Many people who emigrate from other countries to the U.S. come filled with motivation to succeed. Excellent communication and leadership can channel that motivation into working hard and contributing as team members who can accomplish personal goals along with those of their company.

You can exhibit such leadership. You can be genuinely effective in your role as leader, overcoming cultural and language barriers. Follow the formula that I learned the hard way: have fun and create fun for others in your workplace.

Remember that you are unique. Be yourself, and don't feel you must do what everyone else does. Nurture your people and appreciate their uniqueness. They will contribute everything they can in return.

Steve set a great example. The one thing I regret about him is that he never taught me how to cook!

Chapter 1
The Melting Pot that Hasn't Quite Melted

Overview

Identifying problems in the workplace and understanding cultural differences are key to team success in a multicultural workforce. These require an open mind and a willingness to learn about others.

Peter's Story: The Ineffective Manager

Peter was a personable, goal-oriented, well-trained manager in a company that had a good product and great potential. Yet he was *fired*.

Peter was fired because he was ineffective. A number of factors contributed to this disaster, but a major one was his inability to motivate a workforce composed of individuals from at least 16 cultural backgrounds to meet their production quotas. He failed and lost his job.

Peter had moved to San Francisco to take this job. When in his hiring interview he was told that the company's workforce was decidedly multicultural, he believed he would have no problem with that. He even mentioned that he enjoyed foreign movies and both Chinese and Mexican food. He said he would treat all employees equally and with respect, and he did.

Peter was a charming Californian from a "good" family in his late 30s who had earned an MBA at one of the best American universities. He was friendly and tried to chat with the Chinese, Korean, Japanese, Indian, Mexican, American, and other employees who made up his workforce. But he had never traveled outside the U.S. and didn't understand other cultures, which turned out to be his undoing.

First, he talked a lot and very fast and used all the words he had learned while studying for his MBA, which were impressive but not comprehensible to the people he was speaking to. He didn't pay enough attention to notice that they didn't understand him. He didn't ask questions because he assumed they all knew what they were doing or would ask if they didn't, because in his culture, that's what people do.

For example, there was the time when Peter was talking to Tui, a woman from Vietnam, who had asked for a raise during her job evaluation

1

interview. Peter spoke quickly as usual, his sentences liberally sprinkled with big words, telling Tui that she was doing a great job and would get her raise. While Tui tried to listen attentively, she felt like she was being fired at with a verbal machine gun and hardly understood a word that Peter said. When she left his office, she was unsure of whether she would get a raise or be fired.

Peter assumed from Tui's silence and her smile at the end of the interview that all was well, but she was silent because she was trying to find the words to tell him, without being rude, that she didn't understand what he was saying. Her smile was because it was ingrained in her culture that you should smile at the boss if you want to keep your job, let alone if you want a raise.

Being a nice person with good intentions who worked hard wasn't enough for Peter to keep his job, because he didn't understand cultural differences and what they mean in everyday life or how to consider these factors in getting the most from a multicultural workforce. He had no idea how it felt to speak English as a second language in an English-speaking society. He spoke a lot without making sure he was understood—and he wasn't.

Not long before Peter lost his job, I asked him, "How is it going with the workforce? Are you having any difficulty communicating with the different cultures?"

"Oh no," Peter replied. "They're smiling. They're happy. No problem at all."

Peter may have never realized the real source of his failure. He may have decided he wasn't a good manager after all. But the problem was that he failed at the biggest part of a manager's job: motivating the people he managed to produce the results that the company needed.

Peter's Replacement Knew How to Build a Multicultural Team

Someone who understood multicultural dynamics and how to turn that same workforce into a great team replaced Peter. Because of the new manager's approach and procedures, the company grew 300 percent in just a couple of years. The main advantage of the new manager over Peter was an understanding of cultural differences and the special needs of people who struggle with the language, along with recognition of each employee's

2

value and the skill to bring out the full potential of each member of a multicultural team.

Who is responsible for understanding how to work in a multicultural workforce: The manager or the employee?

You could argue that it is up to the immigrants who come to work in America to change themselves and be assimilated into the workforce, to learn the language, and to adapt to the culture. Please understand: They try! It takes time, work, and company leadership that realizes employees' potential; it also takes a manager who appreciates employees for their valuable qualities and will put in the time and effort to break down language and cultural barriers. While there are two sides to this story, in this book we are looking at what managers and companies can do to benefit from a multicultural workforce.

Not every manager who doesn't know how to maximize the potential of a multicultural workforce will lose his or her job. In fact, the issue often goes unnoticed. In many companies, communication between management and the multicultural workforce is so superficial and limited that both sides think that's just the way things are. But if you looked carefully you would see that, while the employees seem to work hard, they really are quite skilled at doing the minimum amount of work required to keep their jobs. They are not contributing their best or coming up with bright ideas that, if acted upon, would quickly increase the company's production and profits. This can mean the difference between 100 percent and 150 percent. Why settle for less than you can get?

Despite communication difficulties, these employees are smarter than others realize. But if nobody asks, cares, or encourages them, why should they try harder? If no one in management takes an interest in their lives, why should they give their heart and soul to the company? If they don't feel included and no one shares the company leadership's vision for the future, their talent and willingness to contribute will lie untapped—a waste of valuable human resources.

Turning that same workforce into a motivated, gung-ho team that is a pleasure to work with is not even difficult. You will learn how to do that from this book. In this first chapter, it is important for you to understand clearly that there is a problem and a great deal to gain from tackling it head-on.

Understanding Different Cultures Is Important

The word *culture* comes from a Latin word, *cultura,* which means cultivation or tending. The *Oxford English Dictionary* defines *culture* as the following:

> 4. The cultivating or development (of the mind, faculties, manners, etc.); improvement or refinement by education and training.

> 5.a. The training, development, and refinement of mind, tastes, and manners; the condition of being thus trained and refined; the intellectual side of civilization.

> 5.b. A particular form or type of intellectual development. Also, the civilization, customs, artistic achievements, etc., of a people, esp. at a certain stage of its development or history.

It is important to understand the difference between *culture* and *personality* or *individuality.* When I talk about *culture* in this book, as in *multicultural,* I am referring to the customs, habits, ways of thinking, ways of behaving, attitudes, work ethics, and mindset of a particular people that are common to the majority of those people and that are instilled as a result of upbringing, training, education, parental example, behavior of the society in which they grew up, and so on. These habits and ways of thinking or acting are deeply ingrained over generations or centuries. They are not easily changed, even if the people who have them want to change them. And why should they?

So when I say, for example, *Japanese culture,* I am talking about the attitudes, beliefs, behavior, and so on of most Japanese people, which they possess by reason of being Japanese and having been educated and instilled with the Japanese way of life, thinking, behaving, manners, approach to life, and such. We certainly would not assume that, if we saw one Japanese man exhibiting anger toward a coworker, all Japanese people have bad tempers. However, if every Japanese person we saw shouted at people in the workplace, we might justifiably think that part of Japanese culture was to wage war at work (this is obviously a fictitious example, as the Japanese are known for the complete opposite in behavior).

> We must clearly distinguish cultural differences from personality traits and individuals' idiosyncrasies.

4

If you know that in a particular Hispanic country everyone is taught that it is immoral to work on Sunday, and you ask your employees from that country to work overtime on Sundays, don't be surprised if you get dirty looks or a mutiny. As a smart manager, you either would know this or find out by inquiring after receiving the first dirty look. You may or may not agree with the moral issue, but that is not the point. If you are going to employ people from that country, you should educate yourself.

Culture is not a matter of skin color or physical appearance. I know second-generation Asian Americans who are definitely American in culture: their behavior, attitudes, and so on, even though their appearance is Asian.

Despite the tremendous diversity in the so-called "melting pot" of America, America has a distinct culture. In some regards, the cultures that formed this country have melted, producing certain attitudes, behaviors, and beliefs among mainstream white Anglo-Saxon protestants that are different from those of their English, Dutch, French, German, Italian, Spanish, and other ancestors. A Frenchman arriving in the U.S. for the first time certainly would see differences between Americans in general and the French back home. Those differences are in culture.

Jinsoo's Famous Apple Story

There's a story I have told so many times to get a point across that it's becoming famous. This story is about a true and seemingly minor incident—not one that could make or break a company or an individual's career, as Peter's career was damaged, but one that makes an important point with a simple example about how people peel an apple.

Having been brought up in Korea, I knew of only one way to peel the skin from an apple: to start at one end with a paring knife and peel around the apple, paring off the skin in one continuous spiral. Ta-da! Peeled in one piece, nice and clean. In Korea, it is important that a refined lady peel fruit in a neat fashion. Older adults may even judge a young woman's readiness for marriage by watching how she prepares and serves a piece of fruit.

Continued…

Therefore, I was surprised after coming to America and working at a particular clothing company to find that not everyone agrees on how to peel an apple.

I had walked into the company's lunchroom and found another employee, Amy, peeling an apple in what appeared to me as a peculiar and even potentially dangerous fashion: peeling the skin in many straight little pieces as if the apple were a carrot or potato.

"What are you doing?" I asked Amy, perplexed at her bizarre behavior.

Amy, who happened to be from China, looked back at me blankly.

"Please stop or you will hurt yourself," I told her. "Let me teach you the proper way to peel an apple."

Because I was Amy's supervisor, she politely watched me demonstrate how I believed an apple should be peeled and even said she would try. But to my dismayed surprise, when she tried to peel the apple as I suggested, she cut her finger. Then she looked at me and said, "Jinsoo, that is not the way to peel an apple. Let me show you how to do it."

Amy then showed me the Cantonese way to peel an apple. But though I was an open person and accepted the various ways people from different countries do things, I could not accept how Amy peeled the apple. Yet Amy insisted that her way was right. I gradually noticed that a lot of Cantonese people peel apples Amy's way; I had just never paid attention before.

While Amy and I were still in the lunchroom, Mary, a Caucasian American, walked in and asked, "What are you guys doing?"

I told Mary that we were talking about the best way to peel an apple. Mary looked at us with a puzzled expression and said, "Why are you spending so much time debating how to peel an apple? I'll show you how."

Mary took the paring knife, cut the apple in half, and took a bite, skin and all.

Amy and I looked at each other in disbelief. Mary was eating the apple's skin!

Continued…

"Wait a minute," I told Mary. "You need to peel the apple. There are a lot of bad things on the skin."

"But the skin is good for you," Mary replied. "You need to eat the skin with the apple."

For another 5 minutes, we stood in the lunchroom arguing about how to peel and eat an apple.

After that incident, whenever any of the three of us saw another one of us peel or eat an apple, we would joke, "No, that's not the way to do it."

"Do it the Cantonese way," Amy would say.

"Do it the American way," Mary would say.

"Do it the Korean way," I would say.

This incident got me thinking about how people often think that their way is the right way and there is no other. While I preferred my way of peeling an apple, Amy preferred her way, and Mary preferred the way of not peeling the apple at all. We shared the goal of eating an apple, but due to three different cultural backgrounds, we had three different approaches, and each of us was convinced that she was right.

I realized that instead of repeating the method we knew, we could consider new ideas and suggestions and gain new perspectives. We could question our beliefs and opinions with the goal of arriving at the best solution no matter where it came from. If we still believe that our way is the best way, we at least needn't try to force our way on others; we can respect their ideas. Amy, Mary, and I gained from our experience. We gained a better understanding of why we believe what we believe and others believe what they believe, and this understanding increased our camaraderie and team spirit.

Manager's Action Plan for Success

- Avoid stereotyping employees based on cultural attitudes, beliefs, or behavior.

- Give a copy of an employee's performance review to the employee in advance of the review meeting so that the employee has time to understand the review.

- Avoid speaking to the employee too quickly. Ask questions politely, giving the employee an opportunity to absorb what you are saying and communicate with you.

- Write and give the employee an action plan for the next six months.

- Recognize that there is more than one way to peel an apple.

Chapter 2
Ignore Cultural Differences at Your Peril

Overview

The amount of untapped talent, skill, and experience going to waste every day in any company that doesn't understand how to get the most from its multicultural workforce is enormous. The loss of positive human contribution and potential is a greater loss than the losses from communication breakdowns that cost a company a large sum of money and threaten its bottom line.

In the apple story, Amy suffered only a small cut on her finger, and everyone ended up laughing. But failing to understand cultural differences can result in serious company losses—including losses of profit, as in the following story.

Vaugh and the Lack of Understanding

Vaugh, a Vietnamese woman, was working as a liaison between a clothing company's design department and its production department, making samples before products went into mass production. Because this woman was so reliable, her boss kept giving her more and more responsibilities in addition to her normal work. The woman never complained, because in Vietnam she was taught to accept whatever came and try to cope.

One day the woman's manager was preparing to ship $1 million worth of products and learned that there were no samples. The clothes could not ship without samples.

"What happened?" the manager excitedly asked Vaugh. "Where are the samples?"

Under such pressure Vaugh finally blew up. "You are giving me too much work!" she responded. "How do you expect me to get everything done? I am only one person. No one could do all you have given me to do."

"Why didn't you tell me?" the manager asked. The manager had assumed that everything was getting done because the woman never gave the manager any feedback to the contrary. It had taken a crisis for the manager to learn that the work simply was not done.

9

"I was afraid that if I said you were giving me too much work you would think that I'm not a capable person," the woman replied quietly.

"But this is a million dollars' worth of product we can't ship because you didn't want to look bad!" said the manager.

The crisis occurred because Vaugh was brought up a certain way and the manager didn't take this cultural factor into consideration. From then on, the manager began paying attention to clues as to how Vaugh might be thinking and feeling and made a point of periodically asking when there might be a problem that Vaugh wasn't talking about. The manager also encouraged Vaugh to communicate issues when they occurred so that they could be dealt with before becoming a serious problem. The incident had cost the company cold, hard cash in reduced profits despite Vaugh's being a highly capable employee. With extra care, training, and development, she became a company star.

The issue is not personality differences or diversity management, which includes race, sexual orientation, and so on. Certainly every employee has his or her own personality and is an individual. The issue is the breakdown in communication, understanding, and trust that can occur due to specific cultural qualities that dictate behavior and attitude, as well as language differences where individuals are struggling to understand and make themselves understood. Culture and language go hand in hand as the two factors that, if not dealt with effectively, can bring about waste or loss of talent and skill that are vital to a company's success.

Tony and the Language Barrier

Tony was a highly motivated and bright young man who worked hard and well and happened to be from Mexico. At the end of one work week before a long holiday weekend, Tony was uncertain of whether his manager wanted him to work overtime through the weekend, which he was quite willing to do, or take the long weekend off. When he asked his manager, the manager didn't give him a clear answer. The manager said, "It'll be a long weekend, so why don't you take a break?"

The manager didn't take the time to explain to Tony, perhaps because Tony was a Mexican and the manager didn't relate to Mexicans, besides which Tony looked a bit rough, that there was a lot of raw material that would be needed urgently after the weekend.

Tony understood his manager to mean that he wasn't urgently needed and should come back after the holiday. When he returned, he lost his job. The manager fired him for not taking the company's needs seriously and taking time off when he was urgently needed. It was a misunderstanding.

Some might think it was Tony's fault for not learning English well enough or sufficiently adapting to an American working environment, or they might think it was just his bad luck and the manager was within his rights to fire him, but that kind of thinking misses the point. The point is that the company lost a valuable, hardworking employee. Tony quickly found another job, this time with a company that was willing to evaluate him not by his appearance or stereotypes but by his abilities and production and that benefited from what Tony had to offer. The loss was to the company that fired him.

If the manager had realized that Tony was intimidated by language and cultural differences and spent a little time explaining the company's needs, as well as making sure that Tony understood, the company would have retained a loyal, smart, hardworking employee who would have made a huge contribution over time. That manager cost the company in production, which translates to dollars.

Linda—Fear of Self-Expression

Situations that arise due to unaddressed cultural issues can border on the ridiculous and might even be laughable if they didn't cost the companies involved so much money.

One company had worked diligently to bring down the rate of returned goods from 8 percent to 2 percent, which saved the $10 million company about $500,000 a year. Then for some inexplicable reason, the return rate rose back to 6 percent. Management checked every possible reason but could not pinpoint what had changed. They even hired a consultant at the cost of $10,000 for three days' work and checked all the procedures but could not find the reason for the returns.

One day one of the managers—a woman successful in dealing with multicultural workforce issues—was in the manufacturing area taking a break. She was approached somewhat timidly by one of the workers, Linda from Beijing, who felt that of all the managers this one probably would be the safe one to talk with. Linda quietly asked the manager if it would be possible to get the lights fixed.

"Lights?" the manager asked. "What's wrong with the lights?"

Suddenly the manager looked up and "saw the light," and the whole problem of returns became crystal clear. The light was so bad in that part of the shop floor that the workers couldn't see well enough to produce the high-quality products that satisfied customers.

When the manager asked Linda why she hadn't reported the problem with the lights sooner, Linda looked into her eyes and explained timidly, "Nobody listens to us. It takes a long time to get attention from the company. Also, I am a shy person. I did not want to make trouble, but the truth is that we cannot see very well."

An American worker or foreman might have just walked up to the manager and said, "Hey man, these guys can't see what they're doing! Can't you get the lights fixed?" But someone who can't speak the language well and feels self-conscious about not really belonging in an unfamiliar foreign environment, someone who has had it instilled into her very being from a young age that it's not polite to complain, isn't comfortable with such a solution.

A program concentrated on making the multicultural workforce into a real team of individuals who felt they were part of the company would have saved hundreds of thousands of dollars in returned merchandise, and who knows how much more in future sales to customers lost because of substandard products.

The cost of not recognizing, acknowledging, and working hard to improve this type of situation is huge. Such situations occur every day in American companies. If you are a manager in a company with a multicultural workforce, such a situation may be going on right under your nose, with you unaware of it.

Wasted Talent, Untapped Skill—The Biggest Loss

The U.S. workplace is packed with people with extraordinary talents and skills whose managers don't understand how to evaluate their education and experience and so do not utilize them to anywhere near full capacity. The cost to U.S. companies can easily be overlooked because those in charge assume that operations are working as well as they can.

They don't realize that the quiet fellow working on the assembly line has an engineering degree and many years of successful experience as a project manager who saved his company in Korea millions of dollars annually by streamlining its production lines. They don't know that the new receptionist with a Spanish accent was the top salesperson in a billion-dollar company in Ecuador for three years in a row and would be highly capable of running the company's entire telesales operation, in which most potential customers speak Spanish better than English.

If you've ever got into a conversation with a taxi driver with a foreign accent and discovered that in his country he was a well-known professor, doctor, or the like, you've probably experienced the feeling: What a waste!

The waste comes from a lack of understanding of other cultures, a failure to communicate and facilitate communication, and an unwillingness to spend the time and money to develop people who don't speak English well and have a different culture. In many cases, the waste is based on a very false economy. The few hours and dollars spent on English lessons, accent correction, and mentoring would be repaid in buckets when the abilities, skills, education, and experience of these people were discovered and put to use.

Know Your Employee: Look Beyond the Language Challenges

A guy named Don came to the U.S. from Morocco and got a job taking care of sales orders and doing order entry. He told the company managers that he wanted to go out on sales calls because he knew he would do well at sales, but the managers thought his accent would make it hard for him to sell and didn't want to train him. His morale went down. He imagined that the managers saw Morocco as a third-world country where no one knew anything. His solution was to leave the company and start his own business, which rapidly became a $1 million company.

On the other hand, a Cambodian physician came to San Francisco and got his first U.S. job working at a fish market. He went to a corporation and applied for a better job, but no one there would hire him because he smelled of fish. He tried a second corporation, where he met a farsighted manager who saw in the man's eyes that he was honest and sincere. After spending some time talking with the man, the manager realized that the man had something special to offer and gave him a creative job in the company (the man easily got rid of the smell of fish: He just took a shower and changed his clothes). Through his creative input, he saved the company $1 million in a year.

It's not difficult to see that someone who was a professional in his or her own country must be capable and competent. Why not use that potential?

Time and again I have seen that the general attitude of a company toward minorities and people whose English is not perfect is set by the CEO and senior management. If the top executives take the time to brief their staff and give the multicultural workforce a look at their vision of the bigger picture for the company, extending trust and communication to include that workforce in the team, the entire company adopts that attitude and reaps the benefits of full cooperation and contribution from everyone: white, black, gray, yellow, or indistinguishable.

However, if the senior managers close their doors and don't let the foreign employees in on what's really going on or treat everyone as part of the team, then there is no team; the workforce will do the minimum that they can get away with, and the company will stumble along like so many other companies whose executives don't realize that in their multicultural workforce is a goldmine of bright ideas, hard work, loyalty, and contribution just waiting to be tapped with a little communication, training, encouragement, and coaching.

People who come to the U.S. from abroad are new to American ways and try hard to learn the language and assimilate a culture that is new and strange to them. In this vulnerable position they feel timid, nervous, and unwilling to stick their neck out; they try to get by without saying or doing the wrong thing. A company's environment either can reinforce their anxieties and confirm to them that they're better off staying quietly in the background or can encourage them to speak up and contribute their creativity and bright ideas for the good of the company.

Consider the large number of highly capable and educated engineers who have come to the U.S. from India. It is part of their culture not to be outspoken about their abilities, but a good manager who understands this will take the time to determine and utilize each individual's skills.

> If you are going to employ people with cultural backgrounds different from your own, you first must understand something about their culture.

14

As a leader, you must communicate with your multicultural workforce in terms they can understand and encourage them to communicate with you, thereby breaking down cultural and language barriers. Then you can talk business and go about utilizing their abilities. Remember that they, like anyone else, love to be challenged and resent being underrated, undervalued, and feeling that their talents and abilities are going to waste.

More and more talented immigrants continue to arrive in the U.S. Don't see them as bringing differences you must tolerate or making it necessary that you follow the laws on equal opportunity employment and nondiscrimination—that is all necessary but very boring. See them enthusiastically as individuals with unique contributions who can make your company grow as well as make it a far more fun environment. Get curious about what makes a Chinese person tick and how you can use that quality to improve the company and its bottom line. Think about how you can channel the energies of the young Italian woman who seems to be bursting with life and emotion into raising the production level of a certain department. Ask the Laotian man what it was like to go to the university in Laos and find out if he learned things they don't teach here, what he believes he's really best at doing.

> Ask questions. Be interested. Communicate. Build trust. Create a fun environment. You'll be amazed at the rewards.

Unlike Peter from Chapter 1, the charming manager who took none of these steps and ended up having to find another job, you will shine in your company and be regarded as something of a magician by turning your multicultural workforce into a valuable, dedicated team. It's not really so difficult. The first step is seeing that there is room for improvement.

Manager's Action Plan for Success

- With daily small talk, gradually build trust over time.

- Never say, "We don't do it that way." Say instead, "I like your idea. Let's talk about it."

- Avoid misunderstandings. Be clear and assertive in your communication.

- Provide employees with motivational classes.

- Become familiar with employees' talents and problem-solving skills.

Chapter 3
A Multicultural Workforce Is a Diamond Waiting to Be Mined

Overview

Following equal opportunity employment practices not only meets legal requirements but also provides a wealth of human resources. A multicultural workforce teems with potential for the organization savvy enough to properly utilize it. When the multicultural workforce reaches its full potential, the organization employing this workforce reaches its full potential as well. Diamonds are waiting to be mined.

The laws designed to prevent discrimination have produced varying viewpoints. Some companies merely tolerate ethnic minorities and those who speak English as a second language, begrudging the government's interference in making up their workforce. Others, however, who are more enlightened and progressive, see in a diverse workforce tremendous advantages over a homogenous one. These progressive organizations actively seek employees from different ethnic backgrounds and encourage them to succeed in their organization, knowing that these employees in turn will contribute and help the company prosper.

If everyone running a company had seen the advantages of employing a diverse workforce, equal opportunity laws never would have been needed. Over the years, I have dealt with so many people from different cultures that it has become clear to me that the advantages of employing a multicultural workforce far outweigh the challenges of language and cultural differences.

It is true that different cultures place emphasis on different abilities, skills, and virtues. Some countries have industries that others do not, with the skills honed in those industries transferable to others. Education varies from country to country. The main differences between cultures in relation to the work environment can be broken down into four areas: experience, education, thinking, and general background.

Businesspeople who have grown up in the U.S. tend to be well-organized managers who are good at strategic thinking. Many have MBAs. They understand how to plan and execute, bring business to the company, run the operation successfully, pay the bills, and handle accounting, tax, and legal issues.

As head of manufacturing for a company that made belts, I made sure that the products sold and ordered were produced with the highest possible quality and shipped on time. I also made sure that workflows were designed for maximum efficiency. I saw how different cultures represented in the workforce played a major role in the company's success, especially with the experience they brought from their respective countries.

For example, one of the belt designs we produced was for braided belts. We were fortunate to have people working at the company who came from Laos, which is well known for its basket weaving; many workers from Laos are skilled in this craft. The Laotian employees made beautifully braided belts for the company.

Likewise, in China there are many sewing factories, and my company employed Chinese men and women with experience in this trade. Even though these employees may not have been sewing belts in their country, their experience proved useful. With retraining that built on their existing skills, they were able to do an excellent job at sewing, which was a major part of our manufacturing process.

At another company where I worked we put a Chinese woman in charge of repair of all garments manufactured. She was extremely skilled and could cut and mend anything. I expanded her job, asking her to come up with better ways of repairing the garments and streamlining operations, and she did so successfully. Her life experience in her native country had been in mending clothes, but we used her knowledge and skills to improve production.

I found that many people I worked with from Hispanic cultures tended to be optimistic and happy. Their disposition seemed to make them well suited for working in shipping and operating machines and equipment. They were often singing and went cheerfully about their work. They were easily motivated toward goals and worked hard to accomplish them.

As a manager, you can look for the strengths of people from different cultures—of course avoiding stereotypes, because in the end each individual is himself or herself—and make the most of them. The result can be an enormous increase in productivity.

Different Cultural Management Styles
Benefit the Company

Management styles vary from culture to culture and country to country and, if utilized, can benefit a company in very real ways. Take Steve, who in his native Hong Kong had owned his own contract company and through it worked for high-end clients in both Europe and the U.S. Unlike some other parts of Asia at the time, Hong Kong was well known for its high-end manufacturing and familiarity in dealing with European countries.

When Steve came to my company as a senior manager, he brought with him his way of dealing with people in a European style. Instead of telling people under him what to do, he asked them. I noticed that he also was especially good at balancing his work with the rest of his life, a common trait among Hong Kong Chinese. He didn't want his people working too hard. He took them to baseball games and often cooked for them. He used food as a means of communication, and I saw how this helped Steve's area of the company run smoothly. Whenever we had a party (which happened every month, when production goals were met), he brought homemade Chinese and British dishes to share. Steve listened to others with a smile, never asserting his own opinion first. He kept an open mind to different ideas.

Steve also brought his experience in working with manufacturing problems in European and U.S. companies, but from the objective viewpoint of a foreign contractor. By knowing what kind of fabrics Europeans liked to use and having familiarity with their manufacturing standards, Steve was immeasurably useful to our company.

Great Ideas from the Team

At one company where I worked, we held a production meeting every morning. Present were a Filipino American, a Mexican American, a Chinese American, and several others from different cultural backgrounds, each with varying degrees of skill in speaking English. We represented many differences: different ideas of what success meant, different ways of solving problems, and so on. But we also had some things in common, and one of them was determination to achieve the monthly production goals we had set. This was vital.

As you can imagine, the obstacles to achieving those goals were numerous, because the goals were not easy. Problem solving was a major factor. Because we were multicultural—the designer was Japanese American, the shipping people were mainly Hispanic, and so on—things tended to be chaotic with so many approaches, but we got the right results because we had a variety of solutions from which to choose the best.

Each Culture Brings Unique Ideas to the Workforce

Different cultures contribute unique aspects to the workforce:

- Kim, a Vietnamese woman, motivated her people in her own way, rewarding them with delicious Vietnamese food when they met their goals, but also yelling at them in her own language when she really needed to get a point across—and it worked.

- Woo, a woman who worked in Kim's department, had kids and often asked others about their kids. Woo took turns with others if they needed to come in late to do something for their kids, always making sure they were covered.

- One employee from Russia was extremely motivated. Even though he had never worked as a braider, he turned out to be one of the best because of his high level of motivation to accomplish his goal.

In the U.S., there is a tendency for people to be highly specialized in their work. For example, software engineers are completely different from hardware engineers. But we should be aware that this is not the case in many countries. Often someone in charge of computer systems handles both software and hardware. There is more room for elasticity, ingenuity, and creative problem solving.

In Thailand, old bicycles are a transportation resource. If you go to Vietnam, you'll see people putting very old tires to use, whereas in the U.S., we would throw them away. But in other places, people think differently. They bring their resourceful approaches to this country, where they can be used in manufacturing.

Every time my company had a problem the employees put their heads together and thought of a solution. These solutions saved the company money and enabled us to meet our production goals.

For example, part of our work was dyeing clothes. We used an expensive method of mixing dye to create a black color, and that wasn't very permanent. Arminio, from El Salvador, looked at our process and said, "Why do you do it that way?"

From experience in his own country, where dyeing is a major industry, Arminio told us there was a different way of doing it. We tried his method and it worked really well. We saved 25% on the cost of dye, *and* the dye was much more permanent. Without Arminio in the workforce, we never would have known about the better method. But also, if we hadn't encouraged him and everyone else who worked at the company to come forward with ideas, to speak up and contribute, Arminio might never have shared what he knew.

Another part of the production process at this company was cutting out tops and bottoms for garments, in different styles and sizes. We cut all the tops from one length of fabric and all the bottoms from another. We used 50 to 60 percent of the fabric this way, with the rest of the fabric wasted. Mina, the Korean American receptionist, saw what we were doing and asked, "Why don't you cut the top and bottom together from the same piece?"

This simple observation, based on Mina's experience in Korea, saved the company half a million dollars a year, all because Mina thought differently. She had been an artist in her country, where she was always working on new shapes. Her idea was a revelation to us, while to her it had been obvious. With her method, we utilized 85 to 90 percent of the fabric.

I always asked the employees, "Do you have a better idea?" I encouraged them to come up with better ways of doing things and never criticized them if their suggestions were not useful.

At another company, a certain part of the manufacturing process was outsourced to Mexico on the grounds that it could be done more cheaply there. One employee, who had been a medical doctor in Indonesia, was able to use his medical knowledge to produce a dye that made it much easier for this particular manufacturing process to be done. He worked out how to make the machines more ergonomically sound. The result was much faster production, so the company was able to bring that part of the operation back from Mexico and do it in-house faster, cheaper, and better. This saved the company millions of dollars and improved quality.

The medical doctor responsible for this improvement was a man I had hired because of his impressive background in his own country. But he had been working at the fish market in San Francisco, and no one else would hire him because he smelled of fish!

Gina, from the Philippines, had been an optician in her native country. She watched the sewing operation in our company and asked, "Why don't you put an individual light in each sewing machine? This will improve visibility and lead to greater accuracy."

She was right. We did what she suggested, and the results were as she promised. The efficiency of the whole department increased, quality improved, and everyone was happier.

Everyone brought a different way of doing things, even when it came to arranging the workflow. With the way things were laid out, it took at least 20 minutes to walk through the entire production line, from start to finish. Then one of our Mexican American employees asked, "Why don't we simplify the layout so it takes only 5 minutes to walk from the beginning of the line to the end?"

This employee had worked in a food-packing plant in Mexico and looked at the production line differently from the rest of us. His suggestion opened our eyes, and we rearranged the workflow so that it speeded up the whole line. Distance was extremely important for efficiency. We also now could see the whole operation from one place, which made the process easier for everyone.

All these improvements came about because of the different viewpoints brought to the table by people of various cultural backgrounds, experience, and training, and because from the start they were all encouraged to contribute their ideas, not to be shy or reticent. It is critical that a manager working with people with limited English skills be particularly careful to ask questions and encourage communication.

The results of doing so speak for themselves.

Manager's Action Plan for Success

- Find out what each individual's culture values: money, excellence, education, promotion advances, humor, or whatever their interests.

- Conduct staff meetings that encourage problem solving.

- Consider and review every idea suggested at least five times with the team.

- Talk with your employees to find out what previous experience they've brought to your company, such as education and work background. You may be amazed that this experience can be your gold mine toward building a more productive department.

- Remember that first-generation immigrants are especially motivated to succeed. Allow them to grow.

Chapter 4

Bring Out the Best in a Multicultural Workforce

Overview

So how do you make the most of a multicultural workforce? What are the points that, if followed, will make a workforce composed of individuals with a variety of ethnic and cultural backgrounds superior to one that is not composed of such individuals? Read on for answers.

Identifying the Wrong Approach

Perhaps the first step in gaining an understanding—and a point of view that will lead to success—is to look at the ways this endeavor can go wrong. This includes how traditionally many companies have addressed this issue erroneously.

The most basic error is failing to integrate the individuals in the workforce into the company as a whole. Perhaps because of perceived language or cultural barriers, management decides that it is too difficult or not worthwhile to include the employee who is studying English as a second language in the company as a whole and just gives him or her a specific task to do, hoping that person will just drive the forklift or operate the machine on the assembly line without further need for attention. This attitude leads to a waste of people, a waste of talent.

Even as a supervisor or manager, I experienced such treatment. My new boss would see me as a smiling, positive Korean American. He or she would glance at me and essentially say, "I'll give you a job. This is what you are supposed to do. Here are the procedures. Follow these steps. Let me know when you are done. Tell me if you need any help."

I never received the message that if I had a better idea or suggestion, I should let my boss know. Every company I worked for practiced the same approach.

For example, one company used a particular Chinese contractor for its sewing. When I took over the manufacturing area, I was told, "Please work with this contractor; we have a good relationship with them. It is important that you work well with them and maintain a good relationship. We respect them; they have helped us a lot."

25

They didn't say, "If you can find someone better…" or "Any suggestions?" They just wanted me to work well with the same contractor and not cause problems.

Based on my experience, I believed that the company could get a better deal. It also seemed wrong that we followed the contractor's production schedule instead of giving the contractor our schedule. We could have told them our strategy and schedule for the entire year and let them fit in with it. After all, they were the contractors and wanted our business. We had the option to get the work done elsewhere. It was only later on, when my company realized I had ideas that could help us produce better quality products while at the same time cutting costs, that I was able to implement the changes I saw were needed. But this came after a lot of arguing on my part, consuming time and energy that could have been better spent.

It is shortsighted for a company leader—or anyone—to assume that the only way to do things is the way they have been doing them, to direct a new employee to stick to established procedures without contributing ideas for better production methods and the like. If your mind is set in stone that the person who has been performing a certain function is the only person who can perform this function and no changes are welcome, you are stuck. You have shut yourself off from the limitless benefits of fresh initiative, sharing responsibility, and the excitement of finding better ways of doing things. One major reason for employing a multicultural workforce is bringing into an organization the variety of contributions that come from different cultures.

Identifying the Right Approach

In my present company, I have a German assistant, Donald. I have learned from Donald that Germans are instilled with a high standard for work and production. I also see from Donald a way of looking at people that is different from the usual perspective I've encountered in the U.S. When Donald looks at people, he doesn't focus on how well dressed they are or how much money is evidenced by their lifestyle. While he does notice these things, he focuses on something deeper: the quality in a person, their personality, individuality, and so on. In the U.S. and some other cultures, we often try to imitate others, but from Donald's German perspective, it is preferable to be different. He also holds a particular respect for women in the workplace. My company is richer and certainly more truly global because Donald is a part of it.

I've seen so many similar yet unique examples. Miki from Shanghai earned an MBA in this country and speaks English very well but is proud of her cultural background and speaks Chinese to her Chinese employees, which helps them feel at home while at work and that they are part of the team.

Kitty is Cantonese and was a schoolteacher in her country before coming to the U.S., so she is patient, skilled at handling difficult people, and meticulous about following procedures. She became an expert at feeding the ego of Enrique from Cuba, who was like a magician at fixing machines but had a macho attitude. Kitty figured out that a simple "thank you" meant a lot to Enrique, and though she sometimes had to remind him to arrive at work on time, with proper management techniques, his worth to the company was like gold.

The lesson we can all learn is that when an employee is struggling with English and a new culture, it's foolish to equate this with a lack of ability to contribute ideas that can benefit the company enormously. At the same time, extra steps must be taken to encourage the employee to overcome any reticence based on these language and cultural difficulties and come forward with ideas. This will bring a high return in personnel investment that is measurable at the bottom line. It will also create a team where each member feels important and proud to contribute.

Management and human resource professionals' unfamiliarity with other countries and cultures contributes greatly to the waste of talent. In hiring interviews, those professionals often ask the candidate only about his or her education and experience *since coming to the U.S.*, totally ignoring their education, training, and work experience in their native country.

When someone of a different culture applies for a job, it is vital to ask about his or her education and experience in his or her native country. Work out with them what training they might need—not only training on the job but also in culture, language, local customs, teamwork, and so on—so they can fully bring to the company the benefits of their education and work experience. It is important to understand now, though, that this is a major omission in many companies that should be avoided.

First Impressions Count—Be Clear and Concise with New Employees

Anyone arriving in a new country and starting work at a new company faces huge challenges; it is vital that management and HR professionals understand this. Initial interviews where company expectations are described stay in the new employee's mind forever.

I still remember my first day at my first corporate job in the U.S. I was told to whom I would report and exactly what I was supposed to do. My job description included no room for initiative or taking responsibility as part of the company. From the start I felt boxed in and that I should not think outside this box.

A company's attitude toward other cultures and a multicultural workforce becomes apparent to the new employee on day one. This is a critical time when the tone is set for the employee's potential value to the company.

If you want to make the most of your multicultural employees, this is how you *must* speak to them from the start: "This is what you will be doing for now. Settle in, get your feet wet, get used to the culture and the company. But we won't forget about you. We will train you so you can move up and grow in this company. We want to utilize your previous experience and build on it."

Give them hope to keep their dreams for this country alive by letting them know that their first position is only the beginning. In six months or a year, you expect them to take on more responsibility. It's essential that you as a leader of the company explain to them that the sky is the limit. Tell them, "We don't want 100 percent of your abilities and talents. We want 1,000 percent." When people come to work for you, show them that you're opening the doors to more than a building.

In your introductory presentation for new hires, don't just explain the company structure, show them where they fit in, and make them feel small. Let them know you understand that everyone comes with different experiences and abilities, and that particularly with someone from another culture and limited English, you may not find out right away what these experiences and abilities are, but they have the potential to go anywhere in the company.

Many employers feel so constrained by employment laws that they're afraid of hiring someone who doesn't work out and then not being able to let them go. These employers may tell their new employees, "OK, you're hired but on six months' probation. We're hiring you to comply with regulations." They never even bother to get to know the person they just hired or recognize what real value that person could be to the organization.

None of my employment experiences in the U.S. began with words such as these: "This is a company where you can develop your skills. We can start you in one department and later move you to others where you've expressed an interest until you find the one that best suits you. From there you can move up and grow. There are no barriers to achievement in this company." Consider the difference between these words and being told you're on probation, the different effects they would produce.

Another thing I heard from employers was, "If you have a problem, tell your supervisor."

Company leaders never invited me to talk to them directly or tell them about my dreams and ambitions. Leaders with this distanced attitude should not be surprised when employees don't care about the company's success, try to blame others for mistakes, and isolate themselves, particularly when they also are challenged with cultural and language differences.

The Single-Culture versus the Multicultural Workforce

The only company I ever worked for that was not multicultural was a textiles company in Korea. Everyone at this company worked extremely hard, a trait common in Koreans. But working at this company was not really fun or exciting. Everything was predictable; we all knew exactly what to expect. After working at the company for three years, each employee received a promotion with a bonus. The future was laid out. Because we all were from the same culture, we ate the same foods. Life was routine and often felt dull.

From working in the U.S. with people born and raised in this country, I can imagine what would happen if I had to accomplish manufacturing goals by managing a workforce made up solely of them: I would never accomplish those goals. Too much time would be spent over arguments about who was right or wrong. This is not so much a comment on U.S. culture as a note that every culture has strengths and weaknesses. That's why bringing together the best of all worlds and minimizing the worst with a *properly led and motivated* multicultural workforce is such a brilliantly workable solution.

Here as in Korea, day-to-day life in a single-culture workforce becomes humdrum and not so much fun. If everyone at the last company I worked for had been born and raised in the U.S., the variety and the interesting cultural differences and life experiences would have been missing. The environment would have been less stimulating, as well as less productive. People would have been stuck in positions based on shortsighted criteria versus character, strengths, and interests. The creative problem solving synergized by brainstorming sessions among people from richly different backgrounds would have gone untapped.

What we had was a magical combination: people from widely varying countries and ethnic groups, each with individual strengths. Some liked to stay late to finish work. Some possessed great persistence in solving problems. Whereas a workforce made up of people born and raised in the U.S. likely would look at the clock, see it was 4:30, say "Time to go home," and start packing up—because that is what they have been taught to do— people from other cultures and countries tend to behave differently. Many from Chinese and Mexican heritage seemed to rely on the company as a major part of their life and so would stay at work till 8:00 or 9:00. I commonly witnessed many employees staying late every day just to finish what they had started, because the accomplishment was important to them. The monthly and annual production and shipping goals at this company *were met every single time* for 10 years straight. We never could have accomplished those goals if everyone had packed up and gone home at 4:30 or 5:00 every day.

People from other countries have extra incentive to succeed, so they try harder. They left their native country to find a better life, often making the sacrifice of leaving their family. They not only want to earn as much as possible to help their family, but they also want to be accepted in their new home, to be successful and able to acquire tangible evidence of their success.

Immigrants to the U.S. also tend to see the wider global aspects of life and work because their experiences have broadened their horizons. And by overcoming the obstacles of functioning in a new country with a different language, they tend to view the seemingly impossible as possible.

At a medical instrumentation company where I once worked, there was a Laotian machine technician whose rate and quality of repair far exceeded that of any of the other technicians, yet no one ever patted him on the back and acknowledged the results of his conscientious efforts. The

30

managers were unaware that a cultural trait for Laotians is expecting and desiring recognition, so the managers treated all the technicians the same. Recognition was so important to the Laotian technician—even more important than his pay—that he quit his job. He was so skilled and efficient that I'm sure he found another job, but because the company was oblivious of cultural traits, it lost the best technician it had. Only the other technicians were happy, because now they didn't look bad in comparison.

More recently, when working on my music CD *Creating Superheroes* with musicians, singers, mixers, and producers of widely varying cultural backgrounds, I got to see how these differences let us come up with unique songs that never would have been created if we had shared the same culture. When the individuals in my musical group work together we generate a particular kind of creativity sparked by our differences. The cross-cultural interaction is magical and extends to more traditional business environments as well.

If during the 20 years that I worked in such environments someone had asked me the questions that I've suggested you ask your employees— what else I wanted to do, how they could utilize my previous experience, what cultural experiences I'd had—they might have realized: She's Korean; Koreans are generally well educated and highly motivated; the company likely would benefit by preparing her for upper management. But then I wouldn't have had to struggle so hard to reach upper management on my own, and I wouldn't be writing this book to help you.

The Multicultural Workforce Is a Fact of Life

As travel becomes easier, cultural diversity increases. The company that views these changes positively, employs such a workforce from the top down, and takes actions to motivate its workforce, mining its talents and potential, will move forward in achieving global success.

A Chinese friend of mine works at a company with a reputation as one of the best and most sought-after places in the world to work. Though my friend has many skills, he has difficulty in presenting his ideas to others— a skill considered crucial at this company. He feels certain that if his company would invest in him by providing training in his weaker areas, such as language and U.S. culture, he would become a tremendous asset to the company and enjoy unlimited success, but his company does not offer this type of training. If this great company is not sufficiently forward

31

thinking to make such an investment in its human resources, imagine what happens at companies not so great.

There is much to learn about motivating different cultures. Each has a different sense of purpose and a different hot button that will energize them to produce and contribute. For many, a title is important. For some, it's the environment. Some want a flexible schedule so that they can take care of their families and personal concerns. A lot of immigrants just hired will say, "I don't care about money. I want to show you what I can do. Then let's talk money."

Often they can double their salary in a year because they've proved their worth to the company.

Many immigrants are good at teamwork. Look closely and you will often see a successful manager, born and raised in the U.S. with pride in working independently, yet supported by a team of immigrants who know how to work together. The manager tells the team what to do but relies on the team for his or her success.

> Investment in training translates to value for money. This is true of all personnel but must be emphasized even more in a multicultural environment.

Don't waste the immigrants you hire because of lack of communication and confidence, or poor leadership. First hire carefully, but then develop this resource.

There's incredible power in a multicultural workforce. It's up to you to bring it out.

Manager's Action Plan for Success

- Be clear in telling the new employee about your promotion procedure when the employee is hired.

- Schedule at least two meetings per year with each employee to relate how they are doing and tell them their status.

- Provide coaching programs to help employees move up to the next level.

- Utilize and build on each employee's previous experience.

- Determine the best incentive for an employee to succeed and give it to them so they will try harder.

- Give the employee responsibility for a small project at first so that they can experience a small win, and then gradually motivate them to take on greater responsibilities for bigger wins.

Chapter 5

Communication and Language: The Key to Multicultural Team Success

Overview

In this chapter, we discuss aspects of communication that need to be addressed when motivating a multicultural workforce—aspects that arise from both language difficulties and cultural differences. We talk about dealing with each successfully.

Communication is the most important element in successfully motivating a multicultural workforce. With good, solid communication between the workforce and management, as well as among the workforce members, trust and confidence grow, responsibility arises—and a team can be built.

Various factors erect strong communication barriers between multicultural workforce members and management, including unfamiliarity with one another's culture, differences between cultures, and difficulties in speaking a new language. One of the first steps the manager of such a workforce must take is making the decision to be willing to give and receive communication for the sake of overcoming such barriers.

Do you remember Peter from Chapter 1? His only real downfall was in the realm of communication. I watched him deal with people from other cultures whose English was poor and saw a disaster in the making, because there really was no communication. Consequently, he had no idea of how the people he was in charge of felt or what they thought. Perhaps because I was an immigrant myself, I could easily place myself in the shoes of the other immigrants who worked at the company.

First Step: Open-Door Communication

When I took over from Peter, my first action was to have my desk moved out of the office—where he used to sit behind a closed door—and set up on the factory floor where I was accessible to the entire workforce. Then everyone could talk to me.

Before I accepted this position, the company's employees had not been given a raise in six years. No one had told management that they wanted a raise, and as was typical, the managers simply avoided communication with the members of their workforce. If they heard any news, they wanted it to be good news.

Every day for six years the 50-member workforce came to work, finished their jobs, and left to go home without saying a word. The workers wanted a raise but couldn't communicate with their managers; they thought they were supposed to just wait, but when no raise came, these people of different cultures grew angry and resentful. Yet they remained silent because they were intimidated by the senior executives and fearful of losing their jobs. It was an artificial situation created by lack of communication.

When I became manager, I instituted a policy of annual evaluations. During these evaluations, the employees asked for a raise and clearly were happy to get something each year, even if only a small increase. Some years the company had to economize and this affected the amount it could give, but I explained this to the employees and they understood. Unlike Peter and other executives, I would not simply avoid the issue. When the employees were brought into management's confidence, they felt that the company's challenges were theirs as well. And because I made an effort to converse with and get to know them, they grew increasingly comfortable with me.

I've seen how some managers avoid one-on-one meetings with employees because they know that such a setting gives individual employees the opportunity to ask for more money, but you simply have to go through that stage. Some supervisors will even withhold from senior management an employee's request for a raise because they want to be sure of their own raise first.

I developed a system whereby each individual employee knew he or she could leave a memo or e-mail message directly for me about anything. I wanted the employees to know that the door was open. Many were concerned that their English wasn't good enough to write a message, so I suggested that they ask a bilingual family member—many had sons or daughters who spoke better English than they did—or a buddy in the workplace to help them. I was careful to always provide enough time to listen. It's crucial to do this no matter how large and fast the company grows.

Second Step: Meal Breaks with Employees

My next step in motivating our multicultural workforce was to start taking meal breaks with my team members instead of with the other company executives. I would sit with one group one day and another the next, and so on, sharing food, talking about them and their cultures and learning about them. I began to see them grow more relaxed and trusting around me, acting as if they felt that I was one of them and not some lofty manager who was inaccessible. They opened up to me about their families, their partners, and their lives away from work. I listened with genuine interest as they talked about their culture—life in Mexico or Thailand or Vietnam. We became friends.

And we started to build a team spirit that would get us through many manufacturing and delivery problems without the difficulties we otherwise might have had. I could see that the members of this multicultural workforce began to feel that they were a part of the company—an important part. They began making suggestions for how company operations could be improved, taking personal responsibility for the company's success.

What made the difference? Communication!

Third Step: Good Listening Skills

In some cultures, people speak slowly compared to others. In my experience, for example, Laotian people tend to speak slowly. On the other hand, in the U.S., people often speak quickly and briefly, immediately getting to the point. The manager easily can become impatient with the length of time it takes for someone of another culture to say something and consequently cut them off without hearing them out, withdrawing attention. This behavior prevents understanding and discourages people from making the effort to communicate further—the exact opposite of what you as manager should be trying to accomplish.

I trained myself to wait patiently until the other person finished talking. I was not going to move a muscle until they finished. I would encourage them to continue by saying "So?" and "And?" and "Do you have anything else to tell me? It's okay to make a mistake." It's important when talking with the individuals in your multicultural workforce that you encourage them to finish what they're trying to say and keep improving their communication.

Communication—and, in particular, listening—is crucial in bringing out people's ideas and helping them find solutions to problems. For example, say someone in the shipping department tells you, "We can't ship $1.2 million worth of product. We can ship only $1 million worth." So you ask why and listen to all the reasons. By asking the person to explain, often you help them come up with their own solutions. They might say, "Well, nobody's working on Saturday or Sunday, so we won't be able to ship by Monday." That's when you might say, "Should we provide lunch to motivate the employees to come to work? Should we offer a bonus?" "Oh, that's a good idea," they might reply. That discussion could solve the problem, making it possible for the company to ship the additional $200,000 worth of goods. And the next time such a problem occurs, that shipper will remember that there are options.

It's always worthwhile to discuss a problem with an employee, to ask them what they think, and to listen to what they have to say. Otherwise they may believe that their authority is limited such that they can't take initiative. By asking helpful questions and listening to the answers, you may prompt the employee to provide a solution.

While any good manager needs excellent listening skills, this is doubly applicable for those working with a multicultural team. Beyond merely being willing to listen, you must encourage employees to talk, express themselves, communicate their ideas and feelings, and finish what they try to say you need to do more than just nod in response. You need to ask positive questions that demonstrate your interest: "How's it going today?" "How does the product's quality look to you?" "Do you need help?" "How did things go yesterday?" Establish a relationship where both sides feel safe to say what they think.

Direct eye contact. Eye contact is an important part of communication when speaking to people in many Western cultures. When you look directly at the person to whom you're speaking, they believe you are being straightforward and truthful. Yet I've met many people who never would look directly at me—they looked at my shoulder or the space above my head but never into my eyes—and I understand this, because in many places in the world, including Korea, direct eye contact is considered disrespectful. I initially experienced difficulty adapting to living in America because of my own cultural conditioning in this matter. Westerners unaware of such conditioning might mistakenly interpret this behavior as evidence of a lack of confidence or honesty.

You can do a great deal to help the members of your multicultural workforce improve their language skills and the confidence with which they communicate in English simply by pointing out, in your day-to-day dealings with them, the communication habits and language usage of the society to which they are earnestly trying to adapt.

Making Communication Happen

Attentive listening and openness in receiving communication are not enough to make it happen. As a manager of a multicultural workforce, you must actively encourage others to make sure that communication occurs. You must look for the places where communication is missing amongst your workforce and remedy this problem when you find it.

One of the supervisors I worked with was especially hard working. He worked in his own separate room where he carefully inspected fabric eight hours a day. But there was a communication problem: he never sent the managers a report, so we never knew how much fabric was inspected and ready for production. One day the fabric cutters needed fabric in order to meet production quotas, but it hadn't yet been passed to them from inspection. This was a major production block.

I went to the fabric inspector and asked where the fabric was.

"It hasn't been inspected. It will take another week," he answered.

"Why didn't you tell us this ahead of time?" I asked, perplexed.

"Because you already told me, no overtime and no hiring," he replied.

What he said was true. I had to explain to him that though company policy was important, meeting production quotas was essential, so judgment was required.

Of course employees should not make unauthorized exceptions to company policy, but they need to know they can communicate to their manager as issues arise. Everyone should be trained to stay flexible and use judgment.

The incident with the fabric inspector was not unusual with this company's members of its multicultural workforce. Often communication that should have happened did not. One likely reason was fear.

Managers need to understand that many cultures, especially those with a strong religious background, function with an element of instilled fear. The people are fearful not only of speaking up in case doing so might get them fired, but also of telling anyone that they have a problem for fear of appearing rude or complaining.

This is where your managerial ability to motivate comes in. By following the methods described in this book, you'll be rewarded with a great team of multicultural employees who care about the company and aren't afraid to speak up and say, "Hey, we've got a big order to fill, so we'd better schedule some overtime in order to get it done on time."

Overcoming Language Barriers—Speak One Common Language on the Job

Overcoming language barriers means using language that will be understood and making sure that one's meaning is clear and gets across.

The employees at the garment company where I worked spoke many languages. We were a "Tower of Babel" and couldn't speak all of each other's languages, so English had to be our common language, yet many workforce members did not speak English well and were reluctant to try. For safety, they leaned toward people of their own culture—a natural inclination, and an obstacle management must overcome when working with people from diverse cultures.

Speaking and understanding English on the job are important. It would be misleading to imply that you can hire a person with any level of English skills—or none at all—and then wave a magic wand that makes them functional in an English-speaking organization where technical skills are required, computer programs and documentation are in English, and so on. While how well a person needs to speak and understand English is something that depends largely on the position you're filling, any English-speaking organization will require a basic minimum level for all employees. Otherwise, they would be courting failure for both the employee and themselves, wasting everyone's time and resources.

The question then arises: How do you determine whether or not a job applicant's English skills are good enough for you to hire him or her for your open position?

Many companies announce job qualifications with a stipulation of three or four years of experience. Yet even when these requirements are met and interviews completed, a company may not wind up with the employee it expected. One reason is that job experience in a foreign country may be totally different from what's considered the equivalent in the U.S. For example, I was an engineer in Korea, but the skills I used in leadership and communication were very different from those expected in a similar position in the U.S.

For a while, we at the garment company made the mistake made by many companies: we assumed that if someone's technical skill was good, their leadership and communication skills would be good as well. But a sound hiring decision should be based on all three abilities.

The answer to the question of how good a job applicant's English must be depends on the position for which they are being considered. For example, if a technically skilled Chinese applicant with minimal English was going to work in manufacturing with a Chinese-speaking supervisor, you should hire the person. Many Asians come to the U.S. with excellent technical skills. Be prepared to invest time and money in teaching English to the new employee. Usually by about six months later, your new hire will have learned the language sufficiently well to perform as a solid team member who will only improve from there.

A periodically completed job evaluation form is a useful tool for quickly revealing who needs extra coaching or classes in English.

Learning English. The smartest managers will hire talented people and then train them to communicate well in English. The best way for a non-native English speaker to become proficient in the language is with a mixture of practicing while at work—speaking English as much as possible with your encouragement—along with formal English classes provided by the company. Such classes may be taken at the local community college at night, or you may even encourage the employee to join a Toastmasters club for six months at the company's expense. Providing an English tutor at the company for a particular employee or group is a more expensive option that tends to be reserved for people in key positions whose rapid English skills acquisition is especially important to the company.

At one company where I worked, I initiated English classes on-site every Friday evening after work. The company paid a teacher to come in and instruct a group of 10 to 20 people for two hours, and then students practiced what they'd learned during the week.

The bonus: employees studying and practicing with each other contributed to good team building and benefited the entire company.

Manager's Action Plan for Success

- Practice an open-door policy: let employees know they are welcome to come to you with issues or concerns and that you will want to help.

- Allow employees to bring a buddy or family member to a one-on-one meeting to help with English translation.

- Take meal breaks at least once a week with employees. They'll love it.

- Communicate clearly. Make sure your staff understands your directions.

- Encourage employees to express their concerns, communicate ideas and feelings, and finish what they try to say.

- Pay attention and use direct eye contact.

- Encourage English as the common language and provide English classes when needed.

Chapter 6
Communication Tips and Techniques to Help Your Multicultural Workforce

Overview

In the U.S., a successful multicultural workforce begins with communicating in the same language: English. This chapter provides tips and techniques for helping your staff communicate and work well together.

Speak English on the Job

While it's best if possible to introduce your company to newcomers in their language, from then on you should encourage everyone to speak English. Because English is corporate America's common language, it's the common denominator you need to bring workforce members together.

Of course employees may use whatever language they choose during break times—you won't follow them around to make sure they're speaking English—but let them know that, when working, using English will help everyone form a more cohesive team and will help them learn the language faster. Explaining your reasoning will meet much less resistance than simply saying, "This is the rule. Follow it."

Help Your Staff Overcome the Fear of Speaking

Speaking before a group of people can be daunting for anyone, but imagine how you'd feel if you had to do so in a language you were just learning. The first time I was invited to speak to an American audience, I was to make a presentation at the Intel Corporation in Silicon Valley—and I was terrified.

I was so worried that no one would be able to understand me, I could barely eat or sleep for a week. I asked my friends to help me practice and also practiced over and over by myself. Eventually my enthusiasm about the motivational topic I wanted to share overcame my fear. By the time my presentation day arrived, I was able to deliver a speech that my audience members' applause and facial expressions told me they understood. This success fueled my desire to continue making motivational presentations.

A manager who is aware of the special challenges a multicultural workforce faces can take steps to ensure that employees learn to improve their skills in presenting ideas, addressing a group, and participating in meetings with confidence. Let them practice presenting their ideas to you or another staff member. Politely correct their pronunciation and vocabulary so that they're able to get a point across clearly.

Effective Meetings Improve Communication and Understanding

One company where I worked instituted daily meetings for its multicultural managers. Every day these managers met with their executive manager and discussed a variety of topics, from their personal lives, including any difficulties they might be having, to production issues, which the meetings helped them resolve.

In periodic sessions with all the company's supervisors and managers, we divided the group in two: One half presented their ideas and the other half evaluated the ideas. The presenters were given three minutes to express their ideas concisely, and the evaluators helped them practice. Presentation specialists coached key personnel one on one. The practice and the coaching, combined with the group activities we conducted regularly, proved highly effective in improving communication and presentation skills.

The company also held monthly meetings for all executives, managers, and employees where the executives familiarized employees with the company's background, and, in turn, the employees were given the opportunity to familiarize attendees with their cultural background. Someone from management might talk about how the company was started. Someone from sales might talk about the destination for the company's products, which happened to be clothing. They might show photo slides of a beautiful window display in a major department store, helping the workforce feel proud of their product and motivating them to do their best in producing the highest quality garments.

These efforts played an important role in breaking down cultural and language barriers and forming the organization into a strong, effective team.

Training and Coaching Programs

The garment company where I worked further exhibited its commitment to team building by investing in courses in English and presentation skills

44

for employees. For many non-native English speakers to become eligible for promotion, such courses, usually requiring 20 hours of study, were necessary.

The company was rewarded by seeing employees' improved communication as well as their appreciation for the company's attention. It's also important that a company providing such training and coaching obtain feedback from the trainees. Ask questions such as "How does the training help you in your job?" and "How can you apply what you're learning to your work?" Don't just pay for the classes and let that be the end of it. A questionnaire can be a useful tool in obtaining feedback as well as providing a record you can later review.

Here's a vital tip for helping multicultural workforce members communicate better: focus on what they're doing right instead of the inevitable mistakes. Remember that negative criticism inhibits free communication. Turn a correction into a positive by asking, "How can we use this example to benefit us next time?"

Toastmasters International — A Speaking Club

What helped me most to become a better speaker — and listener — was joining a Toastmasters club. Toastmasters is composed of people from all walks of life, young and old, involved in a wide range of experiences but sharing one common interest: wanting to improve communication and be understood more clearly. At Toastmasters, members find an opportunity to speak about anything they choose to an audience made up of both native English speakers and those in various stages of learning the language. A fringe benefit is that it's a fun environment. After each Toastmasters meeting I attended, I felt stronger and doubly determined to excel.

I credit Toastmasters as the single most important factor in my becoming comfortable conducting workshops and seminars to large audiences of English speakers. Go to www.toastmasters.org, enter your location, and find out how you and your employees can benefit by joining. I highly recommend it!

Food as a Learning Tool

I learned from my multicultural workforce experience that food provides a common meeting ground for people of all cultures, giving us a basis for learning about one another's cultures and languages. At our lunchroom at the garment company, one day we'd have a Spanish lunch with the Hispanic employees bringing food; another day we'd have Indian food with the Indian employees bringing delicacies to share; and so on. We had fun following the different holidays (for example, Chinese food on the Chinese New Year and American food on the Fourth of July).

Some nights after work we had theme parties. At a noodle party, employees from each culture prepared their version of noodles: Chinese chow mein, Italian spaghetti, Korean and Japanese udong, Hispanic fideos. We talked about the differences in the cultures as well as the foods, each of us learning more about one other.

We all looked forward to these times of relaxation and the pleasure of tasting delicious new foods, times that shaped us as more than an ordinary workforce.

Communicate Company Information with Flowcharts

A company's current operational information and procedures can be most effectively presented in the form of flowcharts viewable either on a computer or on large notice boards. Some companies publish such information in printed manuals and books, but by the time the material is published, often it's out of date.

The successful manager of a multicultural workforce will understand that it's vital to keep the team abreast of what's going on in the company in terms of procedural day-to-day changes and the like. Flowcharts present a visual diagram for everyone to see who is responsible for what job and where everyone fits in to company operations overall. Be sure to keep the charts simple and clear for non-native English speakers.

With the help of such flowcharts, your multicultural workforce members will have a clear concept of the entire production line, with no language barriers getting in the way of understanding.

Specialized Training

At the garment company, we found it most effective to hire individual consultants for getting people up to speed on the technical aspects of their jobs, and we found such consultants readily available. One-on-one coaching always worked fastest, quickly making our team members functional on machine operation, computer program use, and the like.

Often, instructional material for such operations is available only in English, in which case we needed to help some individuals polish their English language skills sufficiently to assimilate the material. At times we did this by sending the individuals to English classes. There really is no substitute for learning the language, and in general, people are eager to do so when they believe it will help them expand their opportunities.

Fong, a Vietnamese employee at the garment company, at first spoke no English and didn't want to do any kind of work that required English skills. The executives, recognizing Fong's potential with the company and that language was her only barrier, offered to send her to English and computer classes, as well as to hire a consultant to work with her one on one. Fong applied her considerable talent to these studies and overcame the language barrier, resulting in her eventual promotion to a position that most companies would pay an employee $100,000 to fill. Because of the company's benefits and investment in her, Fong was happy to take the higher level job at a relatively modest salary, so in the end the company saved money. And Fong's benefits extended beyond those of her job: speaking English to her children at home helped them to excel at school.

Step Up to Your Responsibility

The importance of communication in any workforce cannot be stressed too much. Especially with non-native English speakers, it is critical that you as manager make sure communication has been not only heard or read but also understood. Too many mistakes in a multicultural workforce result from the leader's spending insufficient time and effort in ensuring effective communication. You must step up to this responsibility.

I've found that providing paperwork (for example, e-mail, handouts, or memos) to reinforce verbal communication helps employees understand and remember the message. At the garment company, we asked each employee to sign a form stating that they had read and understood posted information on company policy or instructions regarding production. This might include information such as changes in specifications for items in production—the new spec might be 1 inch longer and 1 inch slimmer for pants, reflecting a change of style, hip size, and so on. Everyone involved needed to know this.

Don't make the common mistake of communicating such information only to supervisors and assuming every member of the workforce will understand.

Go the Extra Mile

A company with multicultural employees can go the extra mile by providing assistance with aspects of employees' lives (for example, health insurance, employment benefits, children's education opportunities, or real estate dealings) that are especially difficult to manage when adapting to living in a new country. At the garment company, we invited provider representatives to present information on their products, often in a variety of languages such as Spanish or Chinese. We helped employees access doctors who spoke their language. We made sure that 401k benefits were clearly understood so that employees knew what they were entitled to.

Communication in a multicultural workforce can be especially challenging, but meeting the challenge results in vast rewards for all concerned. You'll become the leader of a team of individuals who care about the company and gladly excel at their responsibilities, going the extra mile themselves. You'll benefit from their creative ideas for improvement and willingness to work together to accomplish goals. Your company will capitalize on this multitalented, multicultural workforce made up of one person after another who has much to give.

Manager's Action Plan for Success

- Conduct daily and other periodic meetings to improve communication and understanding with employees.

- Provide training programs that teach American culture and business etiquette.

- Institute a weekly Toastmasters club meeting at work during lunch. Encourage the executives and employees to have fun practicing together.

- Begin sharing food with employees. See how quickly you learn about their cultures and languages.

- Use flowcharts to reinforce communication.

- Identify employees with special talents and give them extra training to fill the company's needs.

- Be willing to go the extra mile.

Chapter 7
Understanding Cultural Differences and Work Ethics

Overview

Another important difference among cultures is that each has its own standard of work ethics.

People from Latin American countries such as El Salvador and Costa Rica are ingrained with the belief that family comes first: they consider it normal and important to spend weekend time with family members at parties or other get-togethers. On the other hand, many people from Asian cultures don't mind having to work all night if that's what it takes to get the job done; to them, work is the highest priority because their culture has taught them that success is life's greatest reward. While there are always exceptions—and stereotyping would be foolish—understanding the traits of various cultures in general will move you forward on the road toward most effectively managing your multicultural workforce.

Never make the mistake of companies that lose ambitious people who quit because of a conflict between going to night school to further their education and working mandatory overtime. In fact, something like this occurred at a company where I worked. An Asian supervisor left because her manager thought it was more important for the supervisor to accept a promotion—including more money and responsibility, as well as longer hours—than go to school and get a degree while continuing her current job. The supervisor's family believed that getting a university degree was more important than anything else, and she agreed. She wanted to keep her current position, working hard for eight hours a day but not working overtime so that she could continue her studies. Her manager didn't understand that getting a degree is of primary importance in her culture and continued to pressure her to take the promotion—so she quit.

For many Americans born and raised in this country, part of the work ethic means keeping life in balance. They may want to work hard in their individual way, but not extend themselves while at work to get to know other cultures and their customs.

Cindy was such a person. The manager of the credit department, she insisted on having lunch after 1 p.m. each day, rather than eating when everyone else did at 12:00 or 12:30. At first we couldn't understand why she wanted to eat alone. Finally she told me that at lunchtime she needed peace and quiet and to have that time to herself. It wasn't because she disliked other people. It was simply how she refueled herself.

Another difference between cultures is that some do not practice equality between the sexes, including in the workplace. When you observe and behave sensitively toward such a practice, you will help your workforce members adapt to the U.S. workplace and keep your team functioning optimally.

The Tendency to Separate by Culture

There's a saying that birds of a feather flock together. In many companies, when you walk into the lunchroom, you see people grouping together according to culture: members of each cultural group speak among themselves in their native language. Sometimes you might even feel that they're talking about you. If your organization has reached this point, you have trouble on your hands.

As a manager, you already may have experienced having employees request that only others who share their language and culture work with them in their area.

"May we have only Chinese people working in the logistics department?" you may have heard from some of the Chinese employees already working in that department. Or: "Can we have just Vietnamese working in our department?" Or just Mexicans, or whatever the culture. In my experience, I've found it is a grave mistake to allow this. If you do so, you will never have a team.

Language seems to be the major reason for this preference for separation. When employees in one department come from the same culture, it's especially easy to let this separation happen.

Once a company becomes divided among cultures, the problems begin. For example, Korean grocery stores that employ only Koreans lose customers from other cultures because of the language barrier. I know of an insurance company that employed only Hispanics and, as a result, attracted only Hispanic customers. The Hispanic employees couldn't communicate with customers from other cultures, so the company's clientele was greatly limited. There are countless advantages to having a multicultural workforce.

A company I worked for used to use a Chinese contracting company that was saturated with the Chinese culture. It used a Chinese logo, burned Chinese incense, and employed only people from this culture, who ate the same rice together day after day. Eventually the contractor had trouble building a strong workforce because the employees understood how to work only with other Chinese. Because of its single-culture makeup, the company died.

Companies that are not multicultural often are unnecessarily limited to doing business only with people of their own culture.

When one culture dominates a particular area in a manufacturing environment—say, there are only Indian engineers, or Hispanics have asked to be grouped together in the production area—managers from another culture trying to oversee such groups face major barriers. The group members tend to protect each other and not open up to management, often leading to serious trouble.

The solution to this problem is simple: mix cultures together.

Cultural Customs, Beliefs, and Superstitions

Another factor to consider when managing your multicultural workforce is that global cultures have their own customs and beliefs, and superstitions too. For example, the Laotian New Year occurs in April, and the Chinese celebrate their own New Year as well. Revering these holidays is important to members of these cultures; they might need to go to temple or spend time with their families instead of reporting for work. Islamic and Jewish employees who practice their religions must be able to recognize their holidays, perhaps by using vacation days, but some arrangement must be made. These issues can't just be ignored.

While a company can't let the cultural customs of its workforce get in its way of functioning as a business, there are steps it can take to show it respects these customs. It might establish a newsletter about cultural differences so that everyone can learn about them, or encourage employees to talk about their culture during lunchtime or at parties. I found this to be an innovative and successful approach in raising awareness that enabled every one of various cultures to feel they were part of the team.

51

The company where I worked learned a little too late that the Chinese don't clean a factory the day before New Year because doing so is considered bad luck. When we cleaned the factory as usual, the Chinese employees were upset with us. If we had known about the custom, we would have respected it, even if we viewed it as superstition.

In my own Korean culture, we don't write anyone's name in red because it means death. The number 4 also means death, so we don't use it.

The Chinese like to use red tablecloths at company parties because they believe that doing so attracts prosperity. They also like to hang a light or decoration, and they will give you a particular word that means good luck for you. As a manager, you can decide when emphasizing such beliefs might begin to make the company too Chinese, considering that you want to respect all cultures.

It's good to know that certain cultures don't like casual hugging; it's considered too personal. In Dubai, I kissed a Muslim woman's hand in appreciation but immediately could see that this upset her—her face became red—so I knew I had made a mistake. In some cultures, drinking wine in front of women is a despised practice. You must be careful about such behaviors.

Developing an awareness of cultural customs, beliefs, and superstitions will lead to managing a more harmonious multicultural team.

Avoid Judging People Based on Cultural Background

While it's important to become familiar with cultures different from your own, it's equally important to resist the temptation to stereotype the individuals in a culture. I had a boss, Michael, who made a comment to me, "Oh, I went to Korea, and I saw a lot of Korean people drinking. So you like to drink a lot, right?"

Even though Michael acted like he was joking, what he said made a negative impression on me. It resulted in my rejecting not only his comment but also him.

While there are cultural tendencies, every individual is unique. Because I'm from Korea, people have actually said to me, "Oh, you do Tae Kwon Do, right?" While it might come in handy to have a reputation that would make a potential attacker think twice before attacking me, it's inaccurate to assume that all Asians are involved in martial arts.

Another thing that happens is that people say, "Oh yes, in Asia…" as if Asia was one country and everything was the same throughout it. Asia is made up of many countries, and they are all different.

People who think in terms of stereotypes also tend to decide whether or not they like a person based on their cultural background. They might say, "We don't like to work with Indians," or Chinese, or whatever. Eliminating such stereotyping can be a challenge for you when managing your multicultural workforce. The best place for everyone to begin is with themselves.

Instill Confidence

A manager needs to be aware that people who have emigrated from other countries to the U.S. may have trouble believing in themselves and their worth in this strange new environment where everyone appears to be functioning just fine without them. They may work at a company for 12 years and still think they can contribute no welcome ideas for a better way of doing things. This lack of confidence is intensified by difficulty in expressing themselves. Because people born and raised in the U.S. can have trouble relating to this predicament, it often goes unnoticed.

Help People Grow

It is essential that you be willing to nurture the members of your multicultural workforce to grow. Remember that when they left their native country to come here, they did so with a strong desire to find better opportunities for themselves and their families. They are motivated. Helping them so that they feel they are growing both with the company and individually is critical in applying their resulting vitality to the company's own growth.

Human nature pushes each of us to want to grow and improve. Your multicultural workforce wants to learn about the culture of which they're now a part.

I learned something important from a designer I worked with named Elizabeth. Elizabeth loved attending seminars, and she helped me grow by inviting me to join her at an empowerment seminar to learn about making more money and becoming more confident in dealing with money. I eventually organized my own meetings, seminars, and empowerment courses to help the multicultural workforce in our company, especially in relation to their children and their children's education.

The company's executive management showed the employees that it was interested in their children's growth and well-being. Whenever the employees' children received high scores at school, the employees brought the report cards and test papers to work to show them to me. Such mutual caring makes a workforce feel almost like a family itself.

Many immigrants have no one to talk to or advise them about personal issues such as how to buy a house or relationship problems. I made a point of asking the supervisors and personnel I managed questions such as, "How's your husband?" "How's your wife?" "How are your children?" If the employees you manage are comfortable enough to talk with you about personal issues and ask for advice, give them your honest feedback based on your experience. This will help them a lot.

They may feel challenged by how to preserve their dignity in a new country where they are at a disadvantage, or by knowing how to empower themselves. Any personal coaching you can give them will be helpful. You can touch their lives.

Multicultural issues are tied to uncertainty. People wonder, am I doing this right? Whom should I ask? Does anyone recognize my contribution? Anything you, as a manager, can do to alleviate such uncertainty and reassure the members of your multicultural workforce will be effective in building a strong team. Remember that sincere praise, when earned, goes a long way in helping people overcome their uncertainties.

Manager's Action Plan for Success

- Know your employees' idiosyncrasies, dreams, and goals.

- Create ways to mix cultures. Avoid having the same culture always working and eating together.

- Develop a newsletter and invite employees to provide information on their unique customs, etiquette, holidays, and the like. Soon everyone will enjoy talking with one another about their varied customs.

- Avoid stereotyping cultures. Learn what each individual has to offer.

- Every time you see a job well done, praise the employee responsible for it.

Chapter 8
Building Trust and Rapport

Overview

The trust factor is a major issue in a multicultural work environment. Managers born and raised in the U.S. often have trouble trusting employees from other cultures, and the reverse is true too.

A manager must work extra hard to make sure that members of a multicultural workforce trust him or her. As a manager, you also must be in control of the area of the workplace for which you're responsible. It may seem risky, then, to hand over authority to someone from another culture—someone who may not yet trust you—but if you don't give them a chance to do the best they can, showing that you trust them, they'll never step up. You'll lose out on their potential.

Go Out on a Limb

Almost exclusively, Hispanics staffed the shipping department in a company where I worked. We managers gave them a schedule and trusted them to get the shipments out on time. Our policy was to trust our supervisors and employees until they gave us a reason not to, and this policy worked. Occasionally there are exceptions: we had a Laotian driver who stole cash every time we gave him money for a deposit. Most people, however, respond very favorably to being trusted.

A manager needs to understand that the trust factor is particularly important with people who speak English as a second language. You have to build trust gradually by making an extra effort, giving them the tools they need, working on common goals, and getting to know them. Recognize that they tend to feel intimidated by your position as boss. Until full trust has developed on both sides, they may not give you everything they've got. They may appear somewhat reserved.

Take the initiative and go out on a limb by showing that you trust them, and then be patient in earning their trust. This upfront investment will result in immeasurable dividends—and measurable ones at the bottom line as well. You will have a real team made up of members who put everything they've got into the company—who share ideas for improvement that make the company better. It's a lot of work, but it's worth it.

I'll never forget a woman named Linda who helped me so generously when I was recently arrived to the U.S. and floundering with both language and culture. She was a large-framed American who was a neighbor as well as a coworker. Because I didn't know how to drive a car and Linda didn't enjoy driving, she decided to teach me how to drive her car so that I could drive us both to work. Every morning I practiced my driving by driving us to work in her car. During the drive, she tutored me not only in driving but also in American customs. She explained slang and superstitions that are different here from in Korea. She talked about America's Independence Day and history. She told me about American foods and habits. I learned so much from Linda.

With her generosity, Linda gained my undying respect and my trust. Immigrants never forget the people who help them grow and understand the culture in their new country.

If you want to gain the trust of the individuals in your multicultural workforce, be like Linda. Teach them about your culture, get them involved in meeting the company's goals, and help them feel like they are a part of the team. Help them grow not only as employees but also as people. By making a contribution to positively changing people's lives and helping them think in a higher way, you will gain more trust and respect than by raising their pay or giving them a better title (though don't neglect doing those things when due).

Trust is tricky. Often people can't trust until they've experienced another person's trustworthiness over time. If you do something causing loss of trust, it's hard to recover.

Take the necessary steps to deal with trust and uncertainty issues in your multicultural work environment. Your reward will be a workplace that's productive and fun for both you and your workforce.

When working with different cultures, two-sided trust is especially challenging and vital. My method for accomplishing this was to set the best example I could by respecting each individual.

Trust and Motivation Go Hand in Hand

If the supervisors and employees feel that, even though you are a manager, you are also one of them, they will be much more likely to trust you. When they trust you as their leader, despite seeing that you make mistakes and aren't perfect, they'll follow you. Be on the front lines with them working and helping them solve problems. Eat lunch and take breaks with them, not hidden away in an office far from the action. Talk to them. Ask them about their children and their lives. Make them feel comfortable.

When you help make an employee's life easier or more productive, that employee feels supported and motivated by you. But if you are aloof, segregate yourself from them, and make their lives miserable by demanding too much and understanding too little, they will not trust you or really listen to you. You'll be a leader without a true following.

Manager's Action Plan for Success

- Trust your employees for their skills and work ethics and help them trust you.

- Eat lunch together so that everyone can get to know each other.

- At meetings, get employees involved with the company's goals. Help them feel like part of the team.

- Ask about employees' families and enjoy personal "getting to know you" conversation times with them.

- Never do anything that would break your employees' trust of you, and avoid putting anything negative in writing or e-mails.

- Remember that as you build trust, you also build motivation.

Chapter 9

Make It a F.U.N. Environment

Overview

Plain, simple fun is the most successful ingredient for crossing any and all cultural divides and creating team spirit, no matter what differences and difficulties exist. What is F.U.N. (*fun, unique, nurturing*), and how does it work? How does a manager create a F.U.N. environment where cross-cultural issues take a backseat to unified accomplishment? This chapter answers these questions.

Over the years, while working with multicultural workforces, I developed a practical approach to management that has proven highly successful. It works not only with multicultural workforces but in any organizational setting and for everyone. The method evolved as I worked with the day-to-day issues of a multicultural workforce. I call it F.U.N. management.

F.U.N. management is such a broad topic that I have written an entire book about it, but in this book it is important simply to mention its key factors. They are extremely applicable to the multicultural workforce.

The *F.U.N.* in F.U.N. management is not just fun! F.U.N. = fun, unique, and nurturing. In these three letters—and the words they stand for—lies a valuable formula. The formula will lead to success, both for individuals and the organization that employs them. It also will lead to individual happiness resulting from a great work environment, and to a way for employees and employers to give something back to their community and society as well.

It is the key to success in managing a multicultural workforce.

Why F.U.N. management?

For too many people, work is not fun at all. Their creative talent is wasted. Going to work feels like a grind that must be tolerated so that the bills can be paid. If you ask most people to define *work,* they will not say *fun,* and if you ask them to define *fun,* they will not say *work.* Bumper stickers say, "Is it Friday yet?" And this is the tip of the iceberg.

Because work is what most of us spend most of our lives doing, dissatisfaction with work leads to dissatisfaction with life. It also leads to companies producing a fraction of what they could produce. When cultural and language difficulties are added to an already unsatisfactory work situation, the result is anything but fun.

I've noticed what seems to be a growing consciousness that it's time for change. Some forward-looking companies are trying a new approach. They've begun striving to provide a work environment that is more employee-friendly, and to some degree, such companies are succeeding. In a number of cases, this attempt takes the form of goofiness and comedy in the workplace, which is not really the answer. Other companies try to make the workplace seem like a home away from home, and to some extent, they are making a positive difference. It is encouraging that there seems to be a general awakening to the fact that running a company is not just about the bottom line but must include some responsibility for helping the people who make up the organization have a satisfying, balanced life.

My "Un-Fun" Experience on the Job

I went through a life-changing experience resulting from work environments where F.U.N. management was not present. After emigrating from Korea, I worked my way up to management in several U.S. companies. I believed that what was required of me was leaving my problems at home, coming to work, and being completely serious for eight hours.

Executive management was overseeing me, as I was overseeing my subordinates. I watched a time clock, checked e-mail, and performed other routine duties. I was expected to stay in my work area for those eight hours, other than for my short break at lunchtime.

You know how it is: You must sit at your desk. Your boss is watching. You must think. Attend meetings. Make sure the people working for you are doing what they are supposed to do. Apply the knowledge you acquired in school.

There is not a lot of room for the individual to be creative. There is no provision for human contact that is not stress-related. If employees chat for more than a couple of moments, a supervisor tells them, "This is work time, not talking time." Sitting at a desk for eight hours, seriously focused on nothing but increasing production, stifles creativity.

I wanted to succeed in this country, so I tried to emulate the traditional management style. But while my hard work helped increase company profits, and I earned sufficient money to buy all the material things I wanted, I was unhappy. I could see that the people around me were unhappy as well. This in itself was not enough to make me change, though, because I thought it was just the way things were.

My wake-up call came when I was fired. I was not fired for poor performance in meeting production goals. I was so serious and demanding of the people who worked under me that their complaints reached the people I worked under. The employees said I was mean, and in a way they were right: I didn't care about them. I was fired because I was *no* fun; the people around me could not enjoy their work because of me.

I had taken pride in my work; I had tried to do what I thought was expected of me, and being fired came as a great shock. I was ready to pack my bags and take a plane back to Korea.

I didn't leave, though; I stayed. Gradually, with help and encouragement, I decided to try again. But I knew I had to change.

I determined that I would reinvent myself. I'd become a positive person who was fun for others to be around. I'd use my creativity, enjoy life, and strive to make life more enjoyable for others. I'd give something back to the community.

I worked on myself over a period of time. It felt like going into hell and coming out a different person. Finally I knew I was a new Jinsoo.

I promised myself that when I started my next job, it would be as that new Jinsoo. To prepare, I thought hard about what success really means to me and to other people: What are the truly important values? How could I help not only myself but also others to achieve true success? I knew it was about more than money. It is never difficult to find examples of people with plenty of money that nevertheless are miserable.

Change Is Good

At the next company where I worked, I wanted to put my new plan into action. Managing a production area with a workforce made up of people from 16 different cultures, all with varying degrees of English skills, gave me lots of opportunities. Fortunately, my new company was willing to let me experiment.

I like talking with people and, from my experience in Korea, knew I work better when I have genuine human relationships with coworkers, and I believe this is true for others as well. I decided to begin every workday with a one-hour meeting with the nine or so supervisors for whose areas I was directly responsible.

We shared the answers to questions such as "How was your weekend?" and "How are your children?" The discussions were always informal, and soon we began bonding remarkably well. We talked about production-related matters as well as personal ones, but not in a pressured or stressful way. I kept the mood deliberately light. The result was an amazingly creative multicultural team, where before there had been a group of individuals, each trying to get by with the minimum effort so as not to get fired.

As a group, we decided to change the traditional perspective for dealing with the various problems that arise in any workplace on a daily basis. Instead of finding someone to blame or treating the problem as if it were a matter of life and death, we decided to find a way to make overcoming obstacles fun. While keeping in mind that we needed to help the company to prosper, we saw that when we laughed at our mistakes, we were better able to turn them around. When people know it's safe to make a mistake, they're not afraid to be innovative and try different things, and they learn.

We started having fun! The goals were clear, the rewards for achieving them were substantial, and every team member began to play to win. The company thrived, and so did the individuals. The 16 cultures came together as one team.

I saw how team members blossomed when we gave them training, education, and opportunities in their areas of interest, recognizing and strengthening the skills and talents each person brought and utilizing them such that both they and the company benefited. It is crucial that employees see that their employer views them as people and not as machines. Each has something unique to contribute. With my new attitude, I worked hard to bring out these unique abilities in the members of my team and considered this a major part of my job. This company became my training field for expertise on managing a multicultural workforce.

As trust grew, employees began sharing their personal problems with the group, and as a group we dealt with them. This was the opposite of the traditional "Don't bring your problems to work" motto. It takes only common sense to see that when someone is in the middle of a divorce or their child is in serious trouble, their work will be affected if they have no one to talk to about it. Such problems are intensified for someone trying to find their way in an unfamiliar culture and with limited English skills. I wanted to create a work environment where people knew they would get help if they needed it. Helping each other this way strengthened our team even more.

Together, we built an environment where we looked forward to coming to work and flourished as individuals. We communicated openly, felt proud of our accomplishments, and were rewarded for them.

Employee satisfaction isn't a business's only concern; certainly the business also must thrive financially. But guess what? The changes we made not only transformed employee satisfaction but also improved the company's bottom line—*dramatically*. Product quality improved, drastically reducing the rate of returned goods. And because efficiency increased, production—and revenue—went way up as well. The company subsequently expanded. How strange!

What Is F.U.N. Management?

Let's examine "F.U.N. management," one piece at a time. F.U.N. stands for

- Fun
- Unique
- Nurturing

Here's an overview of the basic concepts; a little later, we'll go into each in more detail.

Fun. Life can be so serious. We might think that people who are the most serious get the most done, but if we look closely, we see that people who are the best at their jobs—inspiring their employees to produce the most— actually are quite playful and light-spirited. These people clearly enjoy themselves, laugh a lot, smile at others, and in general have fun.

If we're going to spend a large part of our lives working, we might as well enjoy it! And we might as well help those around us enjoy themselves too. This way, everyone wins: you, the employees, the company, and the customers.

Unique. Each person is different from every other one. Each has equal value. We all have our own unique personality to contribute. It's a big mistake to try to get employees to conform to someone's idea of how they should be. It stands to reason that the most you can get from a person is the person himself. So instead of trying to force people to change, help them be more themselves.

63

Nurturing. It's a well-known business concept that the most valuable asset of any organization is its people, and this is true. But you won't benefit from knowing this concept unless you apply it in practical terms. To get the most from the people you manage, you must take care of them: help them develop, train and teach them, trust them, and treat them with care. When you do, you'll be rewarded with their loyalty and contributions you couldn't have imagined. The alternative is something with which you may be familiar: employees who show up on Monday morning only because they need the week's paycheck and who spend the week just putting in their time until Friday rolls around.

Please understand that F.U.N. management is not about telling some jokes to get a few laughs. Let's look at each of its elements in greater depth.

Getting Things Done with "Fun"

You might think that if you're having fun, you can't be getting much done, but when you understand how the two can complement each other, you're well on your way to the *fun* part of F.U.N. management. It has nothing to do with everyone standing around goofing off all day. Certainly that would not get much done!

It doesn't take a lot of time to smile, be friendly, or communicate in a relaxed tone of voice in order to keep things light. If you're so used to behaving in a worried and overly serious manner that doing this sounds strange to you, then "fake it until you make it"—it won't be long until your feelings catch up.

I remember how I used to behave at one company where I worked. Whenever something went wrong, the first thing I did was panic. My face would turn into a stiff, serious mask. Then I'd look around for someone to blame! I'm sure that the people who worked for me got to know what to expect from me. If I wasn't smiling, they probably said among themselves, "Uh-oh. She's not smiling. Who's she going to pick on today?" And I'm sorry to say that they would have been right.

As the new Jinsoo, however, I worked with my staff to find another way of dealing with challenging situations. Something awful could happen (and let's face it, sometimes it does), and I would say, "Ooh la la!" This was a signal to the people who worked with me that we had a challenge to deal with; we needed to put our heads together to resolve it *fast*.

And we would resolve the problem, with everyone pitching in, certain that even if it was they who had caused the problem, no one would point a finger of blame. Because we worked together this way, problems really did become fun challenges. We all felt more relaxed, knowing we didn't have to live in fear of doing something wrong. It's hard to do your best when all you're thinking about is not doing anything wrong. This comes from the negative management style.

Be a Fun Leader

Can you think of anyone who, just by walking into a room, can suddenly make everyone there feel good, more comfortable, and drawn to that person as if by a magnet? We call such people *leaders*. Here are the five qualities I've found to be present in a fun leader:

- ability to connect with others
- dedication to personal growth
- feeling alive, energetic, and staying active
- animated facial expressions and expressive body language
- strong sense of humor versus behaving too seriously

How can *you* become this kind of person? Here are my suggestions:

- Make the effort to control or eliminate negative emotional reactions such as anger.
- Cultivate a positive attitude.
- Study inspirational material to nourish your new attitude.

More about "Unique"

Just as each individual is unique, each has a unique contribution to make. People are not "an IBM man," "a Microsoft woman," or even "a typical American manager." We are all really just *ourselves*. The *u* in *unique* could easily stand for *you—you*nique!

I believe that the way of the future will be recognizing each individual's uniqueness. We will not try to be like someone else, such as Bill Gates or the CEO of your company or someone who graduated from Harvard. We will know that the most anyone can be is themselves.

What this means for you as a manager is that you don't have just a "mass of employees." What you have are individual human beings who

65

happen to work for you. If you want to maximize the value of this human resource, you won't treat them as if they are all the same. You'll get to know their different strengths, weaknesses, and needs. And while culture and language are part of their uniqueness, you'll be aware that that's just the beginning. They also have unique personalities.

What you and the individuals in your workforce have in common is a purpose: to contribute your skills toward helping the company succeed so that you all can succeed in turn. It's your job to facilitate communication among the unique members of the team.

Sometimes we get so fearful of appearing to be different in a corporate environment that we start to lose touch with our own uniqueness. Here are some ideas for getting back in touch with who you are:

- Welcome new experiences in all areas of your life.
- Don't imitate anyone else. Be yourself!
- Trust your instincts.
- Remember you don't fail by trying, only by giving up.

"Nurturing" Is Rewarding

If you want people to give you their absolute best, you have to give them something more than a paycheck: you have to nurture them. Just as with anything or anyone dependent on you that you want to see reach their maximum potential, you must take certain steps to help them become the best they can.

Take an interest in them as individuals. Listen to them. Pay attention to their problems. Help them. Use company resources to train them. Be patient. Encourage them. In other words, *nurture* them. Soon you'll see your efforts rewarded.

Don't be like the executives and managers at one company where I worked, whose motto was "Don't bring your personal problems to work. Leave them at home!" The personnel turnover at this company was huge. It was clear to employees that management cared only about meeting immediate production goals; employees were paid to do it, and that was that.

Remember as you nurture the individuals in your workforce that the goal is not to change them so that they're more like you. Value their unique qualities and just help them be their best possible selves.

When you nurture the members of your multicultural team, they will never forget you.

Manager's Action Plan for Success

- Make every day a F.U.N. day at work!

- Build a "1" team. Start every morning with a one-hour planning meeting that's *fun*.

- Find the unique qualities of each employee and encourage them to open up with their individual style.

- Help employees develop and use their special skills to their fullest potential.

- Remember that in a F.U.N. environment, work gets done better and more quickly, so be a F.U.N. leader.

Chapter 10

The Essence of F.U.N.—Success on the Job

Overview

F.U.N. is a different way of looking at not only work, but also life.

- F = *fun*. Fun means laughter, optimism, and openness.

- U = *unique*. Think of individuality, creativity, and originality.

- N = *nurturing*. Nurturing includes self-development, caring for others, and making a contribution to the community and society.

- Fun + Unique + Nurturing = *global success*. For an individual, this can lead to success in all areas of life. For a company—or even a country—it can transcend culture, nationality, and language, and lead to success in the world.

The Meaning of Success

Each of us needs to be clear about what success means to us. As a manager, you also must be clear about what success means to each of the individuals for whom you are responsible. Success doesn't mean the same thing to everyone. Each individual, each organization, and each country has his or her own idea of success.

"Jinsoo, I am so stressed out. I think I need to see a therapist," a friend recently told me, and then she sighed deeply.

This friend had seen me walking on the sidewalk as she drove by in her Ferrari, and she stopped, lowered her car window, and called out to me. I could see from the look on her face that she was stressed and a bit sad, even though she looked beautiful sitting there in what appeared to be a new Armani suit, with the sun glinting on diamonds around her neck and on her fingers. I could see that she had been shopping: her car was filled with expensive-looking bags.

To the rest of the world, this woman is a highly successful businesswoman with an enviable life. She lives like a queen in a palatial estate on 100 acres of rolling countryside in Napa Valley, and she's blessed with a wonderful husband and two great kids. Running her business requires only 15 hours of her time per week; she spends the rest of her time pursuing hobbies—such as shopping at Gucci.

"I don't have any energy," she told me sadly that day. "I wish I were like you."

I sometimes wonder what my friend believes would make her feel truly successful and happy. I know it isn't "the American dream," because she already has that and more. Whenever I see her she looks worried and rarely smiles.

Another woman I know, a Korean woman, won $6 million in the lottery! She had enough money to set herself up for life. When I ran into her soon after she received the news of her good fortune, I was about to congratulate her but then noticed that she looked angry.

"I have to pay 20 percent of my money in taxes," she complained. "I guess I'll have to quit my hairdresser job."

The words I was about to say died on my lips. Suddenly I felt sorry for this woman because she seemed so miserable.

We all know that success means having lots of money, a big house, a family, and expensive cars…right?

Apparently not: according to the two previous examples and others it's not difficult to find. It doesn't automatically follow that if you're wealthy you'll be successful and happy.

None of us wants to be poor, and being well paid for our work is one sign of success. On the other hand, if you hate your job, can you call yourself successful? If you harbor a driving ambition to become a concert pianist but end up selling insurance, no amount of money will make you happy. Or if your family is your top priority but you spend every waking hour doing work that means nothing to you, paying for the expensive house, cars, and college educations for a family that you never have time to see, you've left yourself out of your own dream and got caught in a vicious circle.

The most basic point about F.U.N. is identifying what success means to you personally. Like the definition of *u* in F.U.N., your idea of success will be unique. No one else can tell you what success means because the answer comes from inside you.

Now apply this concept to your multicultural workforce. To manage this workforce successfully, you need to know how each person in the workforce defines success. How can you find out? Ask them!

You'll be surprised at the answers you get. Different cultures tend to value different things. For example, in many Asian countries, education is most highly valued. In other cultures, an impressive title is worth a lot. To Hispanics, the family is highly prized, and family members want to do all they can to help each other.

Stop reading for a moment and think about your own idea of success. What would make you genuinely happy?

For years, my own personal idea of success was based on a stereotype: college degrees; good job with impressive title and high salary; expensive house, car, and so on. But after achieving those things and finding myself no happier than before, and seeing that others who had achieved those things were not happy either, I had to face the fact that the stereotype did not fit me. I had to change my direction so that I was on my own road to success, not someone else's.

To bring F.U.N. management to your multicultural workforce, you need to be on your own road to success. Look first in the mirror. Find a smile there before you start trying to inspire smiles on the faces of others.

F.U.N.—What It Really Means

When you're sure you know what success means to you, you're ready to consider how to achieve that success.

You might have heard someone say, "He's a good Microsoft (or IBM, Samsung, Alcatel, or whatever) man" or "She's a perfect Avon (or Starbucks, Toyota, or whatever) woman." It's all very well that such companies hire people who fit a certain profile, but a company benefits most from its people when each individual brings his or her own personality, individuality, and unique skills, ideas, and point of view. These qualities need to be nurtured, not crushed or molded to conform.

The "unique" part of F.U.N. management (the *u*) really means *you*. It doesn't mean that there should be no organizational policy or that everyone can just ignore the rules and have a state of anarchy. It means that the most successful—and healthiest—operating environment is one where people can be themselves, where they know that their unique contributions are valued, and where originality and creativity are not frowned on but rewarded.

Creativity at Google

Here's a good example. Engineers at Google are instructed that 20 percent of the time Google pays them for is to be spent working on whatever the engineers want to work on. Now *there* is clear evidence of a high level of trust and belief in the individual, and the individual's unique value to the company. Management essentially is saying, "We know that, left to your own devices and without any direction from us, you are going to come up with brilliant ideas that will make this company better."

And that's just what the engineers do. One came up with the idea of Google News, got a few others enthused about the product, and among them they created it.

Laughter Is Fun

Part of F.U.N. management is *fun,* and fun leads to laughter—one of the oldest forms of therapy known. Consider the difference in your reaction if someone laughs at a mistake they just made versus if they get overly serious, blame themselves—or someone else—and take great pains to try to justify the mistake. In the second case, suddenly that mistake becomes much more important than it was to begin with.

Just a smile makes a big difference. Consider how you feel if you walk into your boss's office to talk with her and she looks up from her desk with a smile, versus how you feel if she looks up with a frown and an expression of anger or stress. Even though there may be serious matters to discuss, the smile leads to getting more accomplished. We come up with our best ideas for problem solving when we feel relaxed versus tense and fearful.

I used to feel tense and fearful at my job, and I passed on those feelings to those I managed. I never smiled. The employees were afraid of me. I hired, fired, and walked over dead bodies if necessary to accomplish the company's production goals. Had I not been fired myself, I might never have made the effort to learn that smiling and laughter accomplish more than snarling and growling. People who enjoy working with a manager contribute more than people afraid of losing their job.

Be Optimistic and Open-Minded—Expect the Best

I've discovered that it's more fun to be optimistic than pessimistic, and this attitude positively affects the people around me. When you expect the best outcome, the expectation alone can help that outcome to occur. When you show the people you manage that you have faith in their ability to do an outstanding job, you help them believe in themselves and try harder, not because they are scared or forced but because they feel inspired to do the best that they possibly can. There may be exceptions where this doesn't occur, but if you keep your focus on where it does, the negative results will wither from lack of attention. This may seem like magic, but just try it. It works.

The old Jinsoo went to work every morning anticipating the day's problems, and her expectations were met with a never-ending supply. But the new Jinsoo started looking for the positive qualities in people that she could praise and encourage. And what a difference! The people around her began to shine.

To nurture the unique qualities in the individuals of your multicultural workforce, you need to be open. This is very different from being tolerant, which means putting up with differences. I'm talking about opening your mind to differences: cultures, ideas, customs, and ways of living. Truly dynamic people actively go out and search for differences that stretch them and help them grow rather than staying settled in their fixed ways, with the same ideas and inflexible approach to people, situations, and life. When you are open to the members of your multicultural workforce, they can help you step outside your old boundaries.

Nurturing and Self-Development

Nurturing includes at least three aspects: nurturing self, nurturing the people around one, and nurturing one's community, that is, nurturing on a wider scale.

I can't overstress the importance of nurturing ourselves. It's not about being selfish. We can't be of much benefit to our family, friends, organization, or society if we don't take good care of ourselves.

Self-development includes keeping an open, curious, and interested mind, always learning and reinventing yourself. Learning certainly doesn't end with a formal education. In fact, it's just beginning. In another chapter, I'll tell you what I've done to reinvent myself (my latest adventure is taking small-aircraft flying lessons). I have varied interests that help make life worthwhile and also make me more useful to others.

When you are responsible for others—such as family, friends, or people who work for you—you need to take the best possible care of them. I don't mean treating them as if they were helpless; I mean making sure they are developing, learning, acquiring new skills, and improving. A company that nurtures its employees in this way is stronger than one that just expects people to get on with their work and has no concern for personal expansion.

Once your life is set up the way you want it and you're on the road to success, it's a fairly natural impulse to look around and see where you can give something back to society.

I clearly recall an occasion when I was facing what seemed like a major problem and received help from someone who had no motive other than that he wanted to help.

An executive at the company where I worked told me that I had to give an important presentation—in English, of course—to the entire company. I was a nervous wreck! After hearing this news, I was driving my car down the freeway worrying when I heard an advertisement on the radio for something called Toastmasters. A voice said, "If you want to learn to give public speeches, this is the place to learn." I scribbled the phone number on a piece of paper, called it as soon as I could, and soon was paying my first visit to a meeting of a San Francisco Toastmasters club.

At the meeting, I met a man named Sal Dossani, who happened to own a travel agency. During our conversation, I explained why I had come to Toastmasters, and Sal immediately offered to give me free coaching. I was amazed that he would help me with no remuneration, but that was what he did. He mentored me and showed me how to deliver an excellent speech. My confidence shot way up. If I do say so myself, I gave a great presentation.

That's the kind of selfless gift that you don't forget. When you are in a position to do something similar, you want to be like the person who helped you. Sal's kindness motivated me to set up a Toastmasters club of my own so that I could help others increase their self-confidence and success (more about this in a later chapter).

As unique individuals, we find different ways to give something back to society. It's not the *how* that's important. It's important that we do it. We help not only the community but also ourselves. We grow.

Manager's Action Plan for Success

- Each person has a unique vision for success and happiness. Ask yourself, what is mine?

- Ask your staff, what does success mean to you? What would make you genuinely happy?

- Smile at yourself in the mirror every morning before you go to work.

- Enjoy and acknowledge the unique contributions of everyone at your workplace.

- Welcome laughter.

- Expect the best outcome and then watch how the people around you try hard to make your expectation a reality.

- Take care of your employees' needs; in turn, they will blossom and be motivated to do their best for you.

Chapter 11

Resource Training and Development

Overview

It is time to discuss all aspects of training and developing non-native English-speaking personnel, including what is needed, sample training programs, and determining what resources are available for this purpose.

Training and development is a constant requirement if you want to create and maintain a real team, as well as keep production volume high and quality of product or service excellent. If you want to keep the great team members that you spend so much time and energy finding and hiring, it is crucial that you train them properly.

Remember that everyone wants to learn, grow, and expand. When you spend time, effort, and money training your workforce, improving their skills and abilities, they will trust your intention to take good care of them. They will also feel more like a part of the company and that they are important to it.

Once you have found and hired the right people to work in your multicultural workforce, you need to help them be the best employees they can be with training and development.

There are several ways in which this can be accomplished, and one is not necessarily better than another. Different training and development methods are applicable to different situations.

Overview of Various Types of Training

As mentioned in an earlier chapter, a formal introduction to the company—along with its policies, rules, customs, and culture—is essential. In any organization, large or small—but particularly with a multicultural, non-native English-speaking workforce—this introductory training is key to the long-term success of new personnel.

After the new employee gets to know the company, the next step is on-the-job training. This requires managers, supervisors, or other trainers spending time with each employee, explaining aspects of his or her new job, equipment, work processes, or anything else he or she will need to know in order to do the job. This is also a time for answering questions, making sure the new person knows what he or she is doing.

This aspect of training, which goes on to some degree in any organization, generally is not formally structured. Some managers and supervisors therefore may neglect its importance, thinking they don't have time for anything that doesn't generate immediate production. However, if you want to develop a valuable workforce, you must invest proper training in each member. This is even more important when new employees are experiencing language difficulties and culture shock.

Daily meetings are another aspect of training and development. Depending on how they're conducted, such meetings can be either vital and productive or boring and a waste of time. Employ specific guidelines: managers meet with their supervisors, and supervisors meet with their team. When done correctly, daily meetings are so important in the environment of a multicultural workforce that I have devoted an entire chapter of this book to the subject (see Chapter 13). By the same token, company-wide meetings held less frequently and conducted productively will help build the overall team.

Mentoring can also be used for training, particularly when dealing with varied cultures with language difficulties. The mentor usually is a manager or someone on a more senior level than the new hire, who is given the mentor's contact information, such as e-mail address, so that they can be supported by the mentor for a period of time. The two also meet periodically to discuss any difficulties the new hire has encountered. This resource gives the new hire access to advice on how to deal with unexpected situations and serves as a point of stability while the new employee becomes more comfortable in the job.

ESL (English as a second language) courses and language were covered in Chapter 6. Remember that such courses are vital to every non-native English speaker. The ability to communicate in English is a basic requirement for becoming a valuable and successful team member.

Other types of training include group and personal training, coaching, and specialized training; the latter is for employees who need to learn something particular such as a software program that will get them up to speed on equipment, or who need to acquire a skill needed for their current job or a planned promotion. Outside consultants, trainers, and coaches are the usual resource employed for this purpose; however, online courses are becoming increasingly popular and successful.

Initial Orientation

How orientation is accomplished varies from organization to organization, but usually, there is a handbook or online materials that introduce the company and lay out its basic policies and rules. New hires read this material—getting help, if needed, from supervisors, managers, or more experienced coworkers—and then attest in writing that they have read, understood, and agree to comply with the company's rules, regulations, and policies.

This is not just a mechanical process, particularly where English is not the new employee's native language. Such employees must be helped with understanding what the orientation materials mean. Providing lots of personal attention puts you on the road to helping new hires "find their feet" so that they soon become productive and happy—and content to stay with the company.

In the beginning, training has much to do with showing the new person the company's accomplishments, expectations, maybe a communication chart, and an organizational chart showing who in the company handles what responsibility. Make sure they understand to whom they should go for help, as well as if there is anyone they should not talk to.

Company policies extend to behavior outside the organization, for example, with vendors; such policies also should be clear about employee relations with contractors and the like. At one time, the company where I worked employed many contractors, and we had to specify to the inspectors that they could not accept money or other gifts from the contractors. We met with vendors and instructed them to make sure that their salespeople did not try to buy favors. We needed to determine whether or not we used their products or services based solely on their quality.

On one occasion, a supervisor had to be let go because she accepted a gold ring from one of her employees, to whom she had mentioned that she loved gold. While bribery may be acceptable in certain cultures, we had to get the message across that this is America, and in this country, we don't take bribes.

Another important orientation issue is the company's policy on personal relationships. Business is business, where employees aren't expected to have romantic relationships with their supervisors or go out drinking with them after hours. Also be very clear about sexual harassment.

I had an unfortunate experience with a partner in my own company who happened to be a lawyer. He seemed to be a good fit because he brought experience as an American who had done business in Korea. But one day a customer came to visit us from Korea, and after dinner and drinks, we took her back to her hotel room, where at one point the lawyer started touching her toes. I could see that the customer didn't know what to do; after all, she was Korean and extremely polite. Then the lawyer started hugging her. That was the end of my company's partnership with the lawyer.

Save yourself some trouble by being clear from the very beginning about sexual harassment. Don't just assume people will use common sense.

During orientation time, in addition to telling trainees your expectations and letting them know how they can meet them, be sure to ask for feedback or suggestions. Everyone likes to make a contribution where they work, but particularly with a multicultural workforce, they may not know how best to communicate a suggestion. So be patient; give them plenty of time to persevere and get their point across. Help them become confident in their ability to make their voice heard.

If you want the best quality of diamonds, you cut and polish them with the greatest of care. Believe that *anyone can become anything.* Supervise employees diligently until they become independent.

To summarize, the initial training should let your new employee know what the company expects and how it operates, but at the same time it should give them the freedom to generate ideas for how to improve things. It should let them know they can talk to you and that you will help them determine how they want to develop in the company.

Orientation goes a long way in expressing trust in new employees and, in turn, gaining theirs.

On-the-Job Training

I discovered that the best way to train foreign-born or non-native English-speaking employees after orientation was by using a lot of visual materials, such as well-illustrated manuals and software programs that enabled them to practice what they were learning. In addition, I assigned an individual trainer to them who could help them get up to speed.

The trainer you assign must be someone with sufficient experience to work with the new person one on one and show them the ropes. This phase of training generally takes three or four weeks, depending on the job's complexity.

As manager, you need to ask for feedback from both the trainer and the trainee, meeting with them individually to get each side of the story so that you can determine how the training is going. Make sure that the two understand one another and that the trainee feels comfortable asking the trainer questions.

To encourage this understanding and comfort level, you might suggest that they go to lunch together and talk about the company more informally. Make sure that the trainer you select for this responsibility is a positive person who likes his or her job and exhibits loyalty toward the company. You certainly don't want negative input going from your trainer to your new personnel.

Strangely enough, I once was assigned a trainer who did just that. She discouraged me with comments and questions such as "This is a dead-end job. Why did you apply for it? What's your problem?" She also gossiped about people in the company, telling me this one had a relationship with that one, and she pointed out that someone she saw coming out of the bathroom had white powder on his nose. I persevered in working at the company, but the things this woman said made a negative imprint on my mind. Every time I saw the guy she'd said had white powder on his nose, I imagined the powder.

Before you turn trainers loose on new employees, make sure you train the trainers. Let them know what you expect from them, what you want them to say and do—or *not* say and do. You can get daily feedback from the trainee about what they learned, how they're doing, what else they need, and so on by having them fill out a questionnaire at the end of the day, but don't neglect talking to them as well. Personal contact is especially important in the early days.

Remember that leadership is about knowing what to do when problems arise. As manager, you can be of tremendous assistance in developing employees' positive attitudes. When, in the face of difficulty, you exemplify a positive attitude rather than acting upset and angry, your employees will learn to react this way as well. They'll know that they— and their jobs—are safe and that they can remain calm and upbeat. Then they can figure out how to solve the problem quickly and effectively.

In one company where I managed a staff of supervisors, I spent time with them in daily meetings that included reading positive books with inspirational messages. Though most members of the group were non-native English speakers, we read the books in turn aloud and then discussed the content. We encountered terminology unfamiliar to many group members, but we kept dictionaries on hand in various languages so that everyone understood what was read before we moved on. Sometimes we also walked and talked together.

This activity became so popular that the other managers and supervisors started doing it with the people who reported to them. It took about 20 minutes from the regular workday but yielded rewards beyond measure for the company because workforce members' commitment to the company grew tremendously.

Formal Training

The purpose in training an employee is more than just teaching them how to handle one specific responsibility. You must carefully observe each individual to determine their strengths, their weaknesses, and what they need in order to develop the former and alleviate the latter. Your awareness of this principle will facilitate the company's progress in developing each employee to his or her highest potential.

In a multicultural workplace, two areas in addition to the standard ones need to be considered: English as a second language and cultural training. A variety of approaches may be employed to address these areas, depending on individual needs. You might have classes scheduled that employees attend at an appropriate learning facility or have trainers come to the company and hold classes there. ESL training can also be done on online. For a key individual, you might invest in one-on-one coaching. In my experience, the two most effective approaches are one-on-one coaching and classes for groups of no more than five students.

Cultural training for new employees should include 20 to 30 hours of instruction in which they are shown practical application of information on manners and business culture in general. Usually this is accomplished by bringing a qualified trainer on-site to train groups.

The company benefits tremendously by investing in language and cultural training, eliminating obstacles to realization of full potential from valuable individuals. Much more quickly than they otherwise could have, these employees are participating fully in the company, writing e-mails and displaying other communication and presentation skills.

Employees should be trained in participating at meetings so that they become confident in their ability to make clear, important points succinctly and effectively. I've seen such training—usually conducted by a specialist brought in from outside—pull a team together and result in invigorating, highly productive meetings.

Formal training also is available for unleashing creativity and making work fun. A seminar may be presented by a professional who teaches attendees such skills as brainstorming successfully and productively. Teamwork can be strengthened with such exercises as one where group members write a song together. While this may sound a bit outrageous, I've witnessed its effectiveness in stimulating a desire to work together, resulting in uninhibited creativity and encouraging a sense of fun in the workplace. In addition, music's universality wisely crosses cultural barriers.

I strongly recommend including such creativity training in your formal training program. Such training brings out everyone's former experience and helps them generate new ideas, especially important with a multicultural workforce. The creativity that's stimulated will transfer to business challenges that need to be solved; you'll see your workforce members coming up with brilliant solutions. The cultural diversity itself will stimulate varied viewpoints and solutions that will build on each other.

Help those who are studying English as a second language to practice in the workplace so that they continually improve. For example, if they do a lot of phone work, have someone spend time with them listening to them say what they need to say over and over until they get it right.

In a company where I worked, a customer service representative from Guatemala was great at his job in every respect other than that his English was poor. To address this problem, we composed a series of questions and answers and then coached him on them, and soon we were pleased to see that his English improved dramatically. We decided to go the extra mile and bring in a private tutor for him. As a result, he became our top CSR, effectively managing company relations with our valued customers.

Sometimes you may need to provide training in a culture other than American. For example, a young Russian who managed a number of Chinese employees needed training in the differences between the two cultures. He needed to learn that, whereas in Russia, as in Western cultures, the leadership responsibility is given to whoever exhibits the ability to handle it. In China, it's different. In China, leadership is based on seniority.

In some cultures, you are respected if you are old. In others, longevity with the company is what counts. In still others, it's a matter of whom you know in senior management. After we provided training to the Russian manager in various cultural aspects, he was able to work more effectively with the multicultural employees. Leadership in a multicultural workforce requires its own special training.

When you observe your multicultural workforce carefully, you may see that many people of other cultures feel they cannot be leaders for reasons such as that they are women, they haven't gone to school, they are young, and so on. They believe they are disqualified from leadership. Such a belief is harmful, so it is up to you to prove to your multicultural workforce that it's untrue.

In a company where I worked and found such thinking prevalent, we in management combated this thinking by instituting motivation sessions where everyone read from inspirational books. We also instituted leadership training programs, particularly for our supervisors, who learned they all could be leaders, could come up with new ideas and solve problems—the things a leader does. This was especially key for people who were ripe for promotion.

Leadership training should include use of case studies. Divide trainees into teams, present a problem scenario, and let them come up with solutions. Present situations that could easily happen in your company, for example, say your raw materials are late. The order has to be filled by a certain date, but there's no way it can be done. Ask, "What's your solution? How will you deal with this?" The group sits at a table and brainstorms.

Your objective is to get your potential leaders to use initiative, contribute, discern what you want—to solve problems. They might decide to instruct the salesperson to ask the buyer for an extension or to see if a substitution can be made, or they might look for another fabric source. Leadership training will prepare them for leadership.

Cultural Training

Individuals from diverse cultures tend to have different priorities from one another. Knowledge among workforce members of the different cultures represented in the workplace—their customs, holidays, religious beliefs, how they raise their children, the foods they eat, and so on—

promotes harmony and better teamwork. It also is essential for someone not familiar with the American culture in which they are working to become familiar with that culture sufficiently to feel at home and be able to function.

The answer to providing this knowledge is cultural training. Get a consultant or trainer to come in every couple of months to deliver a cultural training program. Have him or her talk about communication difficulties, leadership challenges, and all aspects of culture. The consultant or trainer will probably call people to the podium and ask them to talk about their culture and the challenges they go through, and he or she will likely talk about various aspects of different cultures that can present challenges and how such challenges can be dealt with. Like taking vitamins, this training needs to be done regularly. You might provide it on an ongoing basis, perhaps a one-hour session each week, rotating various personnel through it.

You can also provide specific training for those who need it. For example, say that a Hispanic employee is dealing directly with customers, many of whom happen to be Chinese. You need to provide the Hispanic employee with training in the customs of the Chinese culture in order for the employee to do the best possible job. This is best accomplished either with one-on-one training or by training a small group of people together who all have the same job requirements. Again, outside consultants are generally best suited for this training.

You might also consider formal cultural training at a local community college. Normally, a company arranges and pays for such training for employees who need it and who likely have a future with the company. It can be quite expensive but is worth the cost.

Most commonly, combinations of different cultural training methods are utilized in successful companies with a multicultural workforce. Training in language, communication, culture, and leadership all are extremely important in the creation and maintenance of a successful multicultural team.

Learning about different cultures in the multicultural workplace should be ongoing and not restricted only to formal training. This can be a lot of fun. For example, if you pay attention to events in different cultures you'll learn that in Laos, New Year's Day is celebrated on April 1. In the best multicultural company I worked for, we had a Laotian employee, Kham, who invited us to come to his temple for the Laotian New Year celebration. This was on a Saturday, and Kham's entire team of around 10 people went together to watch the temple dancing, listen to speeches, and enjoy the food and drinks. For Kham, this was a perfect opportunity to share aspects of his culture to which we otherwise would not have been exposed.

Kham became a great example of how a nurturing work environment can help a foreign individual expand his capabilities in a new culture. When he came to work at the company, he looked like a fugitive from *America's Most Wanted*, but after a couple of years, he came to me one day and said, "I want to show you some pictures." He showed me photos of himself before he came to work for the company and others from after he had been there for some time—and the difference was remarkable. In two years, he'd changed from someone who looked like a fugitive to looking like a CEO, smiling, relaxed, confident, and well groomed. He told me that his family also was doing very well. He clearly was so happy. Life was good for him. It struck me powerfully to see the changes.

Kham was one typical example of how individuals from different cultures thrived in a work environment where they could learn and grow from training and development provided by the company, as well as from the personal care exhibited by their managers. Such care included taking an interest in their personal life, asking if their kids were doing well, making sure they received the help they needed with such endeavors as buying a house, making decisions about their children's education, and so on. As a result of such care, these employees gave back 200 percent to the company, and it showed up on the bottom line.

The company's employees from diverse cultures were proud of their own culture. The Chinese invited us to Chinatown to see how well their kids were doing at their weekend language school or learn their food shopping habits. The Mexicans invited us to their Cinco de Mayo parade and frequently made salsa for us, as well as shared their other foods. We spent lunchtimes together and exchanged cultural information along with food. One man from Southeast Asia brought traditional steamed rice and steamed fish in bamboo baskets—the food was delicious. Sometimes people would line up, begging him, "Do you want to trade your fish and rice for some French fries?" The company encouraged this cultural exchange because it helped build an effective and successful team.

Education was a priority at this company, and as a leader, I encouraged the parents to focus on their children's education. The employees wanted to know about American culture so that they could raise their kids the American way, even though they sent them to Hispanic or Chinese schools so that the children would not lose touch with their own culture. They wanted their kids to speak both languages and live in both cultures. For Independence Day, we put on a traditional American barbecue with ribs and hamburgers, and at Thanksgiving, we always brought in turkey and all the trimmings. Everyone, no matter what their culture, joined in the holiday celebration. The immigrants were true Americans, part of the melting pot. They brought their experiences from their own cultures but drove American cars and bought other American products. They were proud to be Americans succeeding in the USA.

This particular multicultural workforce greatly evolved over time. In the beginning, I saw a lot of cross-cultural antagonism, but as time went on, the company's leaders learned how to motivate the workforce members and bring them together as a team. If your workforce does not function as a team working together, your business cannot succeed.

Mentoring

One-on-one mentoring is extremely successful when done correctly. This works best when consultants are hired to come to the organization but can also be effective when done by managers or others who have been with the company a while *and have a positive attitude toward it.*

Outside consultants come to the company on a regular basis, such as once a week, and in addition may be available by phone or e-mail in case the individuals they are mentoring have questions or need help at other times. They can act as a go-between for a new employee and his or her manager, talking with both to help resolve issues. With an objective listener to whom they can talk about their feelings and any difficulties they're encountering, employees feel supported by a company that wants to help them succeed. Even in a small company, it's a good idea to have at least one person trained in mentoring. In a large company, there should be many more.

I well remember the companies where I worked that had no such mentoring, where there was no one to listen and help. I couldn't talk about my problem of not getting along with someone, so we ended up not saying much to each other at all—not a very healthy environment for any organization where teamwork is of the essence.

In contrast, at another company I had an excellent mentor who helped me through my growing pains and always was there to support me. He continually motivated me and helped me with problems as they arose. This arrangement made a huge difference in my success.

At another company, we had a mentoring program similar to the buddy system. Employees who already had developed multicultural workforce skills mentored those who still needed assistance. Everyone had a person they could go to for help. Such a program has the advantage of the mentor's always being on-site and also of saving the company the expense of hiring a consultant. It's essential with this type of program that plenty of time be spent training the mentors. They need to possess both communication and leadership skills, as well as an appreciation for different cultural values and the ability to be a friend.

Make sure that your mentoring program is not defeated by negative communication from the mentor to the new employee, such as gossip or negative comments about the company and its personnel. The mentor should be fairly senior in the company and speak the language of the person they are mentoring; it's better yet if they're from the same culture.

Mentoring plays an important part in training and developing new employees, particularly in a multicultural environment. You'll soon see how it helps in retaining these valuable individuals.

General Tips and Advice

Stress management. Development and stress management tend to go hand in hand. With non-native English speakers and people not yet fully integrated into the culture, much stress comes from the fact that they don't know what to expect from their future or they feel anxious about it. They want to know what's happening with the company, how they fit into the company's plans, and how well the company is succeeding. Wise company management will provide a forum where senior managers communicate regularly to all employees, ideally as often as every month or two.

At Google, for example, there's a meeting every Friday for all employees at which the founders are present whenever possible, and they answer any questions anyone wants to ask. The Friday meeting is a tradition the company has kept since it was small, despite the enormous logistical problems now involved in organizing such frequent meetings for such a large company. The meetings are worth the effort, though, because they're both popular and effective.

Similarly, at our daily meetings at the garment company, we addressed the question of how to meet our production goal. I also made a point of individually meeting an average of five people in my office every day. I wanted to encourage them and hear what they had to say. It takes this kind of genuine interest in people to mine the company's gold.

Daily communication with new employees. To retain the new people you hire, you or their supervisor should talk to them daily. This takes time and effort, but it can't be neglected. Make sure they don't leave at the end of the day with issues left unhandled that may make today the last time you see them. Ask them daily, "How is everything? Please let me know if you have any problems." You must stay in touch with issues before they become a crisis.

Remind them that we're all human by saying, "Look, I'm one of you. I may have a different colored face or hair, but I'm one of you." People may not believe your sincerity until you prove to them that you care and really are their friend. Do this by communicating, eating lunch with them, and asking them about their families, the country they came from, and so on—not just day-to-day work. Show an interest in their life, their future, their children, and their development as a person. You'll get back 200 percent.

Manager's Action Plan for Success

Following are some of the training programs you can use to help your employees succeed in the company. Choose those that will help your company succeed as well.

- employee orientation and introductory meeting
- on-the-job training
- daily meeting with employees
- daily meeting with supervisors
- mentoring (assign a manager or senior staff member to work one-on-one with an employee)
- ESL or language training on the job, or payment for attending an outside program
- cultural training for new employees
- creative training to stimulate new ideas
- leadership training
- training in specific areas as needed
- community college training
- stress management training

Chapter 12

Motivating a Multicultural Workforce — The Day-to-Day Beat

Overview

Start the day with a positive attitude in daily meetings. Develop common goals. Offer incentives. Become adept at bringing out each individual's strengths.

Broad steps must be taken to motivate a multicultural workforce and keep team spirit high, and you may wonder how this picture unfolds in the day-to-day life of the workplace. What actions must a manager, supervisor, or executive take to ensure that the workforce becomes and remains a genuine, motivated team? This chapter covers the subject in detail.

Keep Yourself Motivated

If you intend to motivate a team—be its cheerleader, set an example, give its members someone they can fall back on—you must keep *yourself* motivated. For a manager or supervisor, this kind of motivation comes from wanting and getting results, from the satisfaction of achieving the goals set for your area, and from maintaining top quality of the company's product or service. It also comes from the enjoyment you feel in being an integral part of a successful team.

In my own experience, I saw the rewards of becoming the unofficial cheerleader and motivator for a large multicultural workforce toward whom no one else paid much attention. To play this part, I needed to make a sharp turnaround in my thinking, because before then I got up in the morning wondering only what kind of problems I would need to face that day—hardly the most effective attitude for breathing enthusiasm into a team. My attitude had to change dramatically. I had to begin the day by asking myself, "How much fun will I have today? How much can I accomplish?"

With such an attitude, you will have the proper perspective for helping motivate others. Start thinking—and really believing—that of course you will have fun today—that fun things will happen. Most managers and supervisors possess the desire to motivate others; if not, they'd be doing a different job. Sometimes that desire just needs to be reawakened.

Sharing Knowledge and Information

To build a motivated team, it is essential that you share company information with the entire workforce. Immigrants, non-native English speakers and those working in the U.S. from other cultures, often feel uncertain about the future of the company and their own role in that future. This lack of knowledge creates a lack of confidence, which in turn results in their being less willing to pitch in and give 110 percent—something they'd be eager to do if they felt secure in their job and confident about the organization's future.

Dysfunction results from top management's thinking that only they need be informed, that there's no need to let anyone else know what's going on, and that they can just issue a stream of orders that may or may not make sense to those hired to execute those orders.

Computer systems have opened a new door to keeping everyone in an organization informed about what's going on. People can use the Internet and intranets to stay abreast of the latest developments and news. Bulletin boards, e-mails, calendars, and the like can be used to help build an informed team. Employees can also get a good idea of how the company is regarded by customers and the general public by paying attention to news on those fronts, but top management should take responsibility for ensuring that everyone working there knows how the company is doing and where it is headed.

Information on annual production goals, how the company stands in relation to these goals at any given time, and what has been and is yet to be accomplished—all this is knowledge that should be freely available to all company employees. They need such information in order to feel they are part of the team, and particularly how their contribution fits into the company's overall production and progress as a whole. They should also be aware of how much of a bonus they'll get if production goals are met or exceeded.

Don't leave people in the dark, as if the company's dealings were a hidden mystery. The result of your openness with them will be a confident and united team.

Goals

Setting goals is vital in welding together a multicultural team. It gives all in the workforce—no matter their culture or language—a common denominator and a personal stake in the company's success. Goals should be set for the year, the month, and the week and also broken down by teams or departments as well as by individuals. They must be posted for everyone to see, such as on a large display board. The goals themselves will depend on the type of organization; for example, in a manufacturing company where I worked, goals were based on the dollar value of product shipped. We also kept close track of returned merchandise as an index of the quality of production and strove to keep the returns number down.

Team members will be motivated by knowing what the goals are, as well as where the teams stand on any give day in relation to the goals. Are they ahead, behind, or right on track?

I've found that when goals are set for the entire organization, with the organization then divided into teams, and each team having its own goal, a degree of competition for the achievement of these goals begins to ignite. Productivity shoots up dramatically. When properly handled, this competitive dynamic provides employees with a lot of fun and helps them look forward to coming to work to achieve their goals.

A word of caution about setting goals: it is essential that when you set a goal, you stay committed to achieving it. Never forget about it. Schedule meetings to inspire ideas and planning. Keep everyone interested in the goal. This way, team members will take on the goal as their own and do everything possible to help achieve it. Respective departments and sections within departments can plan their operations in detail, including tasks such as checking equipment to make sure all is in perfect working order, and verifying that all team members will be present. Team members can be assigned buddies, and if one buddy doesn't show up, the other buddy can call and ask what happened. This way the manager can attend to other duties rather than chase after anyone who might be missing.

Goal setting includes rewarding team members after the goal has been accomplished. Use celebrations, parties, bonuses, trips for winners, and other awards to motivate employees to repeat their success.

Setting and meeting goals is a particularly vital part of keeping the members of a multicultural team working in the same direction with a high morale and sense of accomplishment (in addition to bolstering the company's bottom line). Without goals—or with goals of which only certain people in the company are aware—the workforce in general isn't really going anywhere.

In my experience, I've seen that it's the company's goals that are chiefly responsible for pulling the members of a multicultural workforce together into a real team. Everyone is happy when they meet their goals. Goals enliven the workplace, making it interesting and fun.

Running by the Numbers

When running any organization, particularly one with a multicultural workforce, you must determine strategy based on the numbers—that is, the bottom line. Decisions can't be vague or left to someone's feelings or opinions. When goals are met, the numbers don't lie.

If the goal is $50 million worth of product shipped by June, then at the end of June you can determine if the goal was met by looking at the numbers—how much product was shipped. No one makes excuses if the product shipped was less than the $50 million worth; instead, everyone pulls together to make sure they catch up in the second half of the year. Everyone knows exactly where they are headed. If production was bottle-necked somewhere, they work hard to locate the source of the problem and solve it.

Management based on the numbers gives everyone a clear picture of where they and the company stand, with no room for prejudice, arguments, or excuses.

Parties, Rewards, and Acknowledgment

When people do well at their jobs—when they break their back to meet a goal and give everything they've got to help the team and organization do better—they should be rewarded.

Individuals doing particularly well should be acknowledged publicly. Don't just say, "Oh, Joe has been doing really well recently." Take the time to find out exactly what Joe, or whoever, accomplished and be specific in your praise: "Joe and his team made a very challenging shipping target on time," "Maria came out exceptionally well in an inspection," "Hyun sold $100,000 of merchandise this month," and so on.

When individuals have done a particularly good job, take them to the chief executive's office and praise them to senior managers and executives over the area where they work. Explain what they did.

When other employees see this happening, they're inspired to work for it for themselves. Particularly in a multicultural environment, praise and recognition are extremely important. Since leaving their country, immigrants have been looking for signs of acceptance and recognition. They need assurance that they are doing well in their new environment.

When you've set goals and provided all the tools your multicultural workforce members need to succeed, they will. When this happens, have a party! Make a big deal of major accomplishments. At one company where I worked, annual and monthly goals were set and taken so seriously that we had a party every time we met the goals. We never missed a month. No one on the team would tolerate *not* accomplishing the goal and therefore missing out on the party. Everyone loved the sense of accomplishment along with the fun of the parties, and they encouraged each other because the entire team had to meet the goal, not just an individual. When the company is doing well, look for reasons to have parties. You'll see everyone accomplishing much more than before.

Also have fun celebrating holidays. In a multicultural environment, you needn't look far to find a holiday for one culture or another that everyone can celebrate together. There are Chinese holidays, Laotian holidays, Hanukkah, Christmas, and so on. The parties needn't be big. You can have ice cream parties, barbecues, crab or oyster parties depending on season, pizza parties, and on and on. People love to talk about them in anticipation: "Oh, my company is always having a party." This equates to having a good time at work and makes everyone feel enthusiastic.

For select occasions, you can also have more formal parties, setting tables with elegant cloths and napkins, decorating the lunch room for the occasion, or whatever is appropriate. Afterward, display photos from the party on the notice board. Watch how people enjoy looking at themselves and remembering the party. Such a party can even be held at lunchtime, taking just an extra hour or two. On another holiday you might take the team bowling or to a ball game, or do something else that everyone is certain to enjoy.

Be sure to hold these parties only when the team is doing well. Never reward people who are not producing. Rewards are for outstanding production and accomplishment, not for routine minimal performance. People never really enjoy rewards unless they know they deserve them.

Bonuses and Incentives

The same principle applied to giving other rewards goes for bonuses as well. Bonuses should depend on performance, whether by a team or an individual on the team; bonuses depend on achieving the goals set out. Immediate bonuses are especially effective. If an individual or team does an outstanding job, authorize supervisors to reward them with money or a gift on the spot. The amount needn't be large. It also might be theater tickets or a gift card for a meal at a restaurant or the like. People love receiving gifts as incentives.

At one company where I worked, I was instrumental in increasing production and revenues, and as a reward, every Christmas I received a gift card from a famous restaurant where I took my family. My family and I looked forward to that dinner every year. This sort of bonus encourages an employee to do well year after year as they look forward to the reward for exemplary accomplishment.

In my experience, I've seen that use of rewards and praise is infectious. From receiving praise, workforce members learn to praise each other when they do well. Hard work and high production draw acknowledgment and rewards in multiple ways and on several levels. This even extends to family life: workers who become accustomed to hearing praise for a job well done begin to cultivate the habit of rewarding their children in the same way. A positive behavior pattern takes root.

Monetary bonuses motivate most of us, but remember that different cultures place more or less value on different forms of reward. In some cultures, recognition and acknowledgment may mean more than money.

Take the time to investigate what different individuals consider the highest incentive for working hard and reaching goals. While every individual is different, you will likely find similarities among people of the same culture. Find out what they really want—a promotion, more money?—by asking them.

I experienced difficulty in this country when I worked for an employer who didn't understand that in the country I came from, titles are immensely important. My employer, on the other hand, believed that titles were irrelevant. He assumed that by working extremely hard and helping the company grow, I was looking for more money. He gave me raise after raise, dismissing the information I shared with him that what I really desired was not more money but rather a title. I never got the title I wanted—vice president of manufacturing—until I left this company and found one with executives who were open minded and willing to learn from their employees.

Company leaders must pay attention to what motivates the members of their workforce. With a multicultural workforce, realize that every culture is different. Don't make the mistake of assuming that everyone values what's most important to you.

Handling Problems

To stay motivated, it's crucial that a team's problems be solved as they arise. As leader, you'll find employees bringing their problems to you. In addition to helping them solve any problems they can't solve on their own—for example, with other team members or departments—you'll need to equip them with their own problem-solving skills.

While in a single-culture workforce, the plea "We have a problem here, what can we do?" may often be heard, realize that with immigrants and non-native English speakers, it's different. Such employees may feel so insecure about retaining their job that they're reluctant to bring up problems; they're shy about asking for help. Unfortunately, by the time they do bring up a problem, it may have already become quite serious.

As their leader, you must sit down with them and patiently ask how best they think the problem can be solved. They will likely have thought of a solution but need authorization or intervention from senior management for implementation. Let them make suggestions: they may say this order should be cancelled or another should be extended, or they may propose some other solution that requires your approval and coordination. As the manager, you then can work with the senior manager, sales manager, or others responsible for taking the next action—canceling the order, extending the order, renewing the order, back ordering, or whatever seems best. This is one fairly common example of problem solving.

It's better that you make a decision for handling the problem on the spot, rather than drag it out or put off responding to your employees.

Although occasionally you may make the wrong decision, try to resolve the problem then and there. When you make people wait for a decision, it's easy to forget to get back to them. If this happens, they might be reluctant to ask for help again. They might fear bothering you, or just decide they can't trust you to take them seriously. It's up to you to encourage them to come to you for help, particularly if they appear diffident about voicing problems and ideas for solutions. When you follow through on the information and opinions they shared with you, be sure to tell them that you are doing so and value their input.

Learning

Continual learning is considered a major index of growth and success, particularly by people living in a culture other than their own. By seeing themselves participating actively in the learning process, they naturally feel more motivated to contribute all they have to the team effort.

When you initiate training programs and encourage employees to avail themselves of such programs, you also initiate the rise in team spirit and morale that will result in improved production. At the same time, team members are learning how best to use equipment, complete orders on time, operate computer hardware and software, navigate company systems, even how best to make phone calls, they are becoming more confident and motivated to do their best for you.

Meetings

In my experience, I found daily meetings between a manager and the supervisors reporting to that manager immensely effective. We held this meeting every morning from 9:00 to 10:00, which gave the supervisors, who arrived at 8:00, time to make sure work was going smoothly in their area before the meeting. These meetings took place without fail, no matter what else was happening. In Chapter 13, you'll read more about how important the meetings were and why.

After the daily meeting, the supervisors went to their work area with the motivation and encouragement they'd received from the meeting and shared these positive effects with the people for whom they were responsible. They continued to make sure work was going smoothly, resolved any issues or bottlenecks, and helped solve problems that came up.

It's essential that motivated team leaders in turn motivate team members, including solving mechanical, production, or shipping problems, as well as any other obstacle in the way of achieving the day's goals. For deadlines to be met, ongoing communication and motivation must be present.

Meeting One-on-One

When a manager of a multicultural workforce makes herself accessible to workforce members, it is quite common for its individuals to come up to her and say, "I need to talk to you."

For such a one-on-one meeting, invite the individual to an office where you can talk privately and no one feels threatened. While ideally the meeting with you will include both the individual and his or her supervisor, if the individual prefers to speak with you alone, you will need to report the meeting's outcome to the supervisor so that the supervisor can resolve any issues that remain. Take care not to create a situation in which you become the employee's direct boss, with the supervisor left out of the loop.

When an individuals' English is so poor that they can't explain themselves clearly, let them know that they can bring someone with them who is fluent in both their language and English to translate. You can offer help for their problem only if you understand fully what it is. Sometimes the root of a problem may even come from someone speaking a different language mistakenly thinking that people speaking another language are talking disrespectfully about them when this is not the case at all.

As a leader, realize that you need to take an interest in not just the work problems of the people you manage but the personal problems as well, because the two are intertwined. While it may sound well and good to have a company policy telling people to leave their personal problems at home, consider how realistic this is if someone has just been told that his wife wants a divorce or his child has been kicked out of school—to expect this not to affect his performance on the job is foolish. You cannot realistically expect an employee to work for a company for 10 years and never have a personal problem.

If you ignore such problems when you learn about them, you will later find yourself faced with much bigger ones. Sometimes—particularly with immigrants, who already feel somewhat shaky in their new environment—a personal problem of this magnitude may even cause an individual to quit—to simply not show up for work the next day. Your company would unnecessarily sustain a major loss, and the sudden absence of valuable personnel would affect the entire team. Such upheaval could have been avoided by lending an understanding ear, relieving the individual's pressure by letting him or her know that support and help are available. With this support and understanding, the individual will most likely return to the work area bolstered by your help so that once again he or she can do a great job.

In some cases, personal problems are best handled by letting the employee take vacation time to stay home and resolve the troubling issue. For example, in a company where I worked, a Chinese woman who was key to production was in the midst of a divorce and at the same time going through difficulty with her daughter, who was experiencing a problem with her eyesight. Executive management decided to tell the employee to stay home until these problems were resolved, and in the end, this took three months. At first the employee believed she couldn't possibly take the time off with the heavy workload she had, but management found someone trustworthy to help cover her job while she was gone, and the situation worked out fine for all concerned.

Another employee wanted to have a baby but, most likely due to stress, had experienced three miscarriages. The company's executive management insisted that she take a year off, have her baby, and then return to work when she was truly ready. The company held her job and gave her leave-of-absence pay.

The company's shipping supervisor contracted AIDS at a time when the disease was extremely rare. He kept getting sicker and sicker but tried to hide it from us. We finally persuaded him to tell us what the problem was, and when he did, we kept him on staff but reduced his hours to an amount he could handle. Sadly, this employee eventually died, but in the time he had left, he continually showed his gratitude and loyalty to the company for extending help and understanding to him when he needed it.

A key manager, Steve, who was Chinese, was diagnosed with terminal cancer. After he told executive management, we assisted him in any way we could, such as dealing with health insurance issues. As Steve's illness progressed, he came to work for fewer and fewer hours. He told us that he loved the company so much that he wanted to spend the last of it training others to do his work when he was gone.

Every organization has its own approach to dealing with its employees' personal problems. In my experience, a company that determines to take care of every employee to the best of its ability is most successful. This approach builds loyalty and trust. In such an atmosphere, everyone witnesses how people with problems are helped. They feel confident that, if their time comes to need help, they'll get it. They're happy to give everything they can to the company, without reservation.

Steps for Motivating an Unmotivated Workforce

At this point you may be wondering, "What can I do? I'm already managing a multicultural workforce that definitely is *not* motivated." The signs you see are clear: employees come to work, put in their time, talk very little, and obviously are not giving 100 percent, much less 110 percent. You have trouble finding new people to hire, production goals are unmet, and there's an atmosphere of dissatisfaction.

If this is your situation, there are steps you can take to help change things.

First, look at the numbers. Examine the total output, sales, and gross income—that is, the contribution employees are making. If production is low, it follows that morale will be low too.

Next, examine job descriptions and a production flowchart. Determine whether employees either don't have enough work or are overloaded. Sometimes you'll find that employees are unmotivated because, no matter how hard they work, they never can finish all the work they've been assigned to do. Not having enough to do is equally frustrating. Using a flowchart will show you how much work the teams and individuals have been assigned and whether this amount of work is realistic.

Finally, sit down with the entire team and discuss the situation. With the information you've already assembled at hand, ask everyone what they think is at the bottom of the problem and what specific challenges they're facing. Then add this last piece of information to the rest to solve the puzzle.

From my experience in working with a multicultural workforce, I generally found the reason for low motivation, team spirit, and morale to be one of three things:

1. They find the work uninteresting or have been given too much or too little to do.

2. They have personal problems and don't know how to talk to someone and get help.

3. They're experiencing difficulty in a work relationship with one or more coworkers.

Certainly there may be other causes as well. It's up to you to meet with the individual, discuss the situation, and pinpoint what's wrong.

You may discover that an employee is unhappy with the job he or she has been assigned. In this case, you can ask what other job the employee might like to do and possibly move him or her accordingly. Determine what additional skills might be needed in order for the employee to do the new job or the current job better. Remember that if employees are learning, they will more likely be interested and keep morale high.

If you find that an employee is overloaded with work, you'll need to revise the balance of work on the flowchart, adjusting the workload to fix the problem. You may need to add an assistant for them.

When the problem is rooted in a personal problem or conflict with a coworker, deal with it on a one-to-one basis as covered earlier.

Next, take a look at the goals you've been setting. Make sure there are daily goals with which employees are familiar so that they know what's expected of them that day; do this on a weekly, monthly, and annual basis as well. Strongly encourage the entire workforce to meet these goals. You might encourage enthusiasm by announcing which team and individual have shown the best performance to date. Monitor performance by numbers so that there's no room for opinion—just facts. Look at how many phone calls were made, how many pieces of product produced, sales volume, number of finished product assembled—whatever most accurately reflects accomplishment. You might use an evaluation form as a useful tool.

You'll see that people on multicultural teams can be highly competitive and motivated by competition. They'll do their best to help the team. Handled correctly, this characteristic can raise productivity over the roof. Just make sure that the spirit of competition remains friendly—you don't want to create internal warfare. Divide teams fairly and hold the competition to a manageable scale.

When other problem issues have been dealt with, you can go further in motivating your workforce by taking a look at how pleasant the company's physical surroundings are to work in. Is your workplace one that people can look forward to entering every day, or does it make them want to stay at home? Executive management should support the workforce by creating surroundings that are a pleasure to work in.

As manager, you deal mainly in communication with supervisors, senior management, customers, contractors, vendors, and so on—all types of communication that will help the company achieve its production goals. Particularly in a multicultural environment, you may be approached by individuals who need help in resolving various issues. You must be constantly on watch to ensure that the people for whom you are responsible are getting the training and anything else they need to do their job well.

You must also act as a liaison between employees and senior management. This communication goes both ways. If there are complaints from employees, you must relate them to upper management so that, if valid, they can be corrected. On the other hand, upper management may ask, "Why aren't the employees working harder?" You may need to explain, for example, the learning curve involved. Sometimes senior managers may even object to hiring non-native English speakers because of the communication difficulty. To build your multicultural workforce, you'll need to present a good case for it.

Executive management may believe that in the long run it's better to hire people with strong English skills even if their technical skills are weak. To equip yourself with the best employees for the job, you may need to convincingly explain that a non-native English speaker proves his worth rapidly once the language barrier is removed.

For a time, you may need to speak for the immigrant who is shy and reticent to speak for himself. It will be your job to help him overcome this problem and to prevent misunderstanding between such employees and management. In addition to your communication skills, rely on the production numbers to prove that your workforce is worth the company's patience and investment.

Organizational Health Check

When dealing with multicultural issues, it's vital that you check regularly on how the organization is doing. This is best done with a workforce survey. Give each employee a questionnaire to fill out, assuring all of them that their responses will be kept confidential and no one will be penalized for what they say. Ask how they think the company is treating them, how well cultural matters are dealt with, whether they're experiencing discrimination, and the like.

In addition to this survey, which may be done every six months or so—and more often if deemed necessary—you must take care to stay open to communication from all employees and listen attentively to what they have to say. A continual process of feedback will enable you to adjust your programs accordingly, as well as deal individually with situations that arise.

When you follow the pointers in this chapter for managing a multicultural workforce on a day-to-day basis, you'll find yourself leading a real team of individuals who contribute all they have to the organization. Morale will be high, and company goals will be met regularly because *everyone* on the team considers it their business to meet them.

Manager's Action Plan for Success

- Identify ways to keep yourself motivated on a daily basis.

- Share company information with employees. Let them know what's happening.

- Set goals as a team and follow through on them.

- Reward the team when members reach their goal.

- Meet regularly with employees to help solve any problems that might prevent the team from reaching goals.

- Provide training programs to keep employees motivated.

- Hold one-on-one meetings with employees when needed, especially with unmotivated staff members.

- Remember that personal problems can affect job performance. Stay in close enough touch with your employees to recognize when such problems arise, and then help them by offering understanding and possible solutions.

- Periodically pass out an "Organization Health Check" questionnaire. Keep answers confidential but use the information you learn to improve the organization.

Chapter 13

The Daily Melting Pot Meeting

Overview

The single most effective action I've witnessed for managing a multicultural workforce is holding a daily meeting.

"Daily meeting!?," you may think. "Everyone *hates* meetings."

But hold on. This is a different kind of meeting from any you're likely to have attended. So set aside any meeting phobia you may have developed over your work life and get ready to learn about a new kind of meeting, one that's more than just a "nice to have" activity. This kind of meeting is vital (and also nice to have).

During the eight years when I managed a multicultural workforce, I met with my nine supervisors from 9 a.m. until 10 a.m. every morning without fail. Work started at 8 a.m., so the supervisors had an hour to get their departments rolling before the meeting. The meeting was for the supervisors and myself only, and though it took place in a formal conference room around a large table, the atmosphere was always casual and fun.

These meetings were a combination of elements: part "happiness check"; part training time; part going over production issues, goals, calendar coordination, and brainstorming; and part a daily dose of inspiration. If you've ever attended meetings you couldn't enjoy and felt were a waste of time, you would appreciate the difference of our morning meetings. Everyone who attended loved them and praised their effectiveness.

After the first few meetings, some of the other managers complained that we were spending too much time chatting and having fun. Anyone could see through the windows that we often laughed and smiled, though the meetings certainly had their serious moments as well. Some outside the meetings had trouble understanding why they might overhear us talking about family situations or what we'd done on the weekend. To them, this seemed a bit too relaxed for work.

But the meetings continued, and I'll tell you why.

Before I started holding the morning meeting, the company was getting a return of goods as high as 8 percent and often didn't ship items on time. But after a while, thanks to the meetings and other team-building activities, returns dropped to 2 percent—saving the company $500,000 per month. During this same period of time, the company also managed to close its off-shore manufacturing facilities and bring all production home, so goods were manufactured in the U.S. for less than it had cost to do so abroad.

Sales skyrocketed from $2 million to $4 million, and then to $10 million. Everyone was happy, including upper management.

It was clear that the morning meetings were the single most important factor in bringing about these positive changes. So the meetings continued.

Meeting and Melting

I would get the ball rolling and then we would go around the table, with everyone having their turn. Every single person shared something with the group every single day. "Oh, I went to Chinatown and bought vegetables," one might say. Then another might respond, "What kind of vegetables did you buy?" and so on. On Saturdays, many of the non-English-speaking parents took their children to language schools, so on Monday mornings we'd ask, "How are your children progressing in their language classes?"

We learned from the Cambodian supervisor that April 1 is New Year's Day for Cambodia. We asked why they celebrate the new year then and how they celebrate. He responded by saying, "We celebrate by going to temple and then drinking beer all night," or some such answer. We learned that though we came from different cultural backgrounds, we had a lot in common. In this way, over time, some true "melting" started to occur in our morning melting pot.

At the same time that we talked about personal activities, we were doing the "happiness check"—people made suggestions and offered each other practical help with personal situations that otherwise could have affected their work. Of course we weren't offering legal counsel, but we shared our objective perspective and the best advice we could think of, as well as our caring attention. For example, we learned that someone's daughter had started going out with a new boyfriend, and the supervisor was worried about whether or not this guy was good for her daughter. So someone suggested, "Why not invite him to your house for dinner so you can meet him?" When someone said, "My son isn't going to school," the others provided helpful ideas for solving the problem.

We made a point of encouraging people to speak up if they had problems outside work that we could brainstorm about. It can be particularly hard for immigrants who are not yet adjusted to the U.S. and having difficulty with the language to deal with normal human problems at the same time. We showed them that the company valued their work and depended on them. It was both practical and humane to practice this policy, and we proved that it worked.

Francine, who came to the U.S. from Venezuela, shared with us during one of our meetings that she was having serious problems with both her husband and her health. Though it was very much against her cultural nature to discuss personal problems with those outside her culture at work, with our encouragement, eventually she became comfortable enough to talk more about these issues. We took up the problem as a group and arrived at a solution: everyone agreed to take on part of Francine's job. Although it was a heavy shipping month, we worked together and covered for her, while she went off to get well and sort out her life. I assured her that her job would be waiting when she returned.

After six weeks, Francine did return. She had successfully resolved her personal problems and also completely recovered her health. She felt extremely grateful to the company and continued to work there for more than five additional years, an extremely valuable member of the team.

Francine's contribution to the company more than made up for the six weeks she was absent. But without the meetings, she probably never would have shared what was wrong or been given the time off; her problems likely would have led to her being fired or forced to quit, with her life going downhill and the company losing a valuable employee without understanding why. Though not all situations involving personal problems are so dramatic or require heroic measure to resolve, Francine's case is not an isolated incident. The company's employees came to know and trust that they could get help if they needed it. When the trust factor increased, team spirit and company success increased as well.

One of the goals for the morning meetings was to make people feel comfortable with each other and sure of themselves. Frequently, people working in a place outside their own culture suffer from lack of confidence. While many are highly skilled, talented, and hard working, they may have been trained from childhood to wait for their elders to tell them what to do. It took much effort on management's part to get such employees to feel sure enough of themselves to make their own decisions.

Kim was a good example. She was an excellent assembler who had worked for the company for a long time and worked twice as fast as anyone else because she was so focused. Still, Kim felt unsure of herself and needed a lot of mentoring. It is in such a situation that praise proves its value. Stay sensitive to the fact that highly conscientious people require very light correction if something isn't done right; they respond much more favorably to praise.

Think of people as trees. When you give a tree nourishment, water, and sunlight, it grows. If it is an especially good tree, it grows and grows. Kim was like that—a good tree. At the morning meetings, Kim and others who did something outstanding to warrant praise and support were recognized bountifully. This helped them to overcome their lack of confidence and enabled them to further succeed.

Kim had been entrusted with a supervisor job despite objections from some in the company who pointed out that she had not even finished high school in her own country. But others saw that she was twice as fast as anyone else in the assembly department; she knew what to do and just needed support to boost her confidence. When she got that support, she knew she was trusted. Once people know they are trusted, they can do anything; they begin to shine, as Kim did. Kim's success was another byproduct of our daily meetings.

Then there was Kevin, who came to the U.S. from Russia. Kevin brought with him some great talents: he knew how to keep his area of a facility clean and was highly organized; he helped other people with computer work; he was extremely kind; and he had strong leadership abilities. But Kevin also brought with him a strong Russian accent and a hot temper. The accent was a problem because he had to spend a lot of time explaining things to the employees he managed, and even then nobody understood fully what he was saying. And when he lost his temper, it certainly was a problem. Yet aside from those two disadvantages, he was exceptionally good at his frontline manager's job and loved it. His positive qualities outnumbered the disadvantages.

In one of our daily meetings, Kevin brought up the problem with his accent and asked if he could get some help. The group discussed the question and came up with the idea to hire an accent correction coach, and it was a good thing we did, because soon Kevin's communication improved tremendously. The temper and intolerance took more effort on Kevin's part, but once his improved language skills helped him feel more comfortable and accepted, these behaviors improved too. Kevin was an unquestionable asset to the company, but had it not been for the morning meetings, his contribution too might have been wasted.

The personal time spent in the meetings wasn't great in size but brought everyone together and helped weld—or "melt"—us into a team. It enabled us to understand one another.

Departmental Production Issues

After sharing personal matters in the daily meeting, we moved on to discussing work-related issues. This was when each person brought up any problems occurring in their department; for example, someone might say that buttons kept coming off or seams were pulling apart, or maybe there were holes in the fabric, or after the fabric was dyed, it was shrinking too much. Someone might bring up a problem related to shipping, supplies, design, or anything else affecting a particular aspect of manufacturing that needed to be resolved. Because all the supervisors were present, the problem had to be fixed by one or more of those sitting around the table—there was no escape!

After someone from each department presented their issues, everyone else could ask questions or make comments. I said nothing during this part of the meeting. I had put the group together but wanted its members to voice and resolve their issues with one another's help, not a pronouncement from me. Someone might say, "David! You could have done better" or "David, where were you when all this was going on?" David then got his chance to explain: "Well, I did that, so I don't understand what caused the problem. Maybe it came from Mary's department." Without any interruption from me, the supervisors sorted out and resolved the issue, including coming up with a good idea for preventing it from happening again.

No one in this group was afraid of admitting mistakes, because no one ever was blamed or made to feel badly. Once they had worked out what had gone wrong, they all pitched in and determined what needed to be done and who would do what to remedy the situation.

Every issue was dealt with in this way. It was amazing to me to see how many issues came up and then to imagine how they would have gone unresolved without the meetings. The result of the morning meetings was a much more streamlined organization.

The following incident evidences just how powerful such meetings can be in solving company problems.

One morning, Alice, a production supervisor who came from the Philippines, brought up a serious situation that was threatening production in a big way.

"Last night," she said, "we dyed the garments red, but they came out white!"

Everyone looked around the table at everyone else in panic. We only had one week left to get this shipment out, and the fabric— which was supposed to be red—had all been cut. It would take two months to get in more fabric. What could we do?"

Someone asked Gam, the supervisor of the fabric department, "How come you didn't test-dye the fabric?"

"We were so rushed that we did only a shrink test," Gam replied. He didn't know what to do; in fact, no one knew what to do. The fabric we'd been sent turned out to be a polyester mix instead of the 100 percent natural fiber needed to take the dye.

I spoke up only to say, "Let's try to calm down and think about it. Remember that we always find a way. Let's refuse to say we can't solve this problem."

After a few quiet moments, Mai, the Vietnamese overseer of the design department, began to speak. She pointed out to us that, at this time of year, white clothes were in great demand. Perhaps, she suggested, we could just wash the cut white fabric, complete it as an order of all white garments, and ship it that way. Perhaps we could wait to dye the next batch red.

Mai's simple solution saved the day. I knew that all the managers working together never would have come up with a better idea. Thanks to the morning meetings, we saved all 500 garments at $25 per garment. More importantly, we maintained our usual excellent customer relations. This happened because the supervisors were encouraged to think freely and felt energized and motivated by the morning meetings.

Continued…

Mai, who had been brought up by her parents to think of problems in terms of solutions, received a bonus for her idea. Her pride from this recognition, as well as her example, in turn, helped to motivate others.

This is just one of many similar incidents where issues, large and small, were dealt with successfully in our daily meetings.

By the Numbers

Our morning meetings were very "numbers oriented"; that is, we always came back to the numbers: dollars and cents, number of items shipped, value in dollars, and the overriding point of general agreement—the monthly goal. Everyone agreed that, no matter what, the monthly goal must be met.

Each person's responsibilities were clear. Monthly, weekly, and daily goals all were posted for everyone to see. This was written with dollar signs as well as quantities to be produced, so no one was in doubt about what they needed to do. Any problems anyone had with meeting their goal was brought up at the morning meeting and addressed. The supervisors never left the meeting with the problem unsolved. They knew exactly what to do.

A conversation might go like the following.

"This month we need to make $1 million. That's $250,000 per week. Today is the 15th, and we should be at $500,000 but we're only at $375,000. So what's going on?"

"Oh the fabric…" or a contract problem, or whatever.

"Okay, how will you get it up to $750,000 by the end of the week?"

Then they would sort out the problem and say something like, "We'll come in early every day until we catch up," or whatever their solution. But that monthly goal would be met, no matter what. Because everyone participated in solving the problem and agreed on the solution, reaching the goal was a result of real team action. And as the goals kept getting met, the company kept growing.

We were all focused on the same thing: reaching the goal. It's very straightforward. You must be specific. Use the numbers. Everyone brainstorms. Culture isn't the issue. The goal will be met regardless of anything else.

Everyone brought to the morning meeting the information on what their area had accomplished the day before. We looked at where we were at that point of the month and determined what had to be done in terms of tangible items we could count each day. For example, if we needed to ship $1 million worth of goods that month, 250,000 garments needed to be folded. We broke that down to determine how many garments needed to be folded every day. If 4,000 garments needed to be folded per day, we needed to determine how many people should work on this task. If we got behind in the number of garments folded per day, we needed to determine how to solve this problem: Did someone need to work overtime? Did we need to hire extra people? Everything depended on the numbers. The supervisors knew how to analyze the numbers. This was a language everyone present understood.

In addition to reaching our periodic goals, we understood that the company had an overall goal: to improve every day. At our morning meetings, we worked toward this goal as a team.

Just as the goals were clear, so were the rewards for reaching them. For example, the supervisors might have been promised that, if they made $1 million that month, there would be a cash bonus for each of them as well as a company party. Everyone had something to look forward to.

Inspiration

For the final 10 minutes at the end of every meeting, we would read together a motivational book, such as *The Power of Intention* or *Beyond Positive Thinking*. One person read aloud in English, broken or otherwise, three or so pages, and then we discussed what was read.

Alternatively, we might go over materials on communication, asking one another such questions as, how do you speak to others? How can you motivate them? How can you be a good leader? How can you unstick your mind and be more flexible? Or, how can you absorb energy from the universe?

The inspirational books were so popular with the group that members would read them outside the meetings and even borrow them to take home and read with their families. In this way, they developed a deeper understanding of positive thinking and why they should never say, "I can't do this" or "This is driving me crazy." They learned a better approach: "We have challenges today. We can meet them."

This was a completely new kind of motivation in the workplace for the supervisors. And because it was the final part of the meeting, they always left in a positive frame of mind.

A manager from any cultural background can conduct such a meeting with his or her multicultural workforce. I can't stress its importance too strongly.

In addition to the morning meetings, once a month the entire company met. This gave the senior managers an opportunity to share information about such things as how they started their careers, as well as for employees to talk about their experiences in Hong Kong, Mexico City, or wherever they came from. These meetings lasted for a couple of hours and were held before lunch. They helped the individual employees see the big picture of where the company had come from and where it was headed. The meetings also helped senior managers, from the CEO down, to stay in touch with all their employees.

Meeting Template

Following is a pattern you can follow for holding a daily meeting. Be sure to apply the basic principles given in the earlier part of the chapter.

Example: Daily Meeting Agenda Template

A. Ask what's going on for each individual—both personally and with their team.
- How did yesterday go?
- What's happening with each function today, this week, this month?
- Who needs what from whom (how can you help each other)?
- What do you need from your manager to succeed (help, knowledge, skills, resources)?
- Give recognition for success and improvement.
- Periodically celebrate success.

B. Make sure they are tracking goals.
- Set goals that are easy to understand.
- Make sure everyone is aware of the goals.

Continued…

113

- Review the goals for today, this week, and this month.
- Ask how each person is doing in regard to the goals.
- Require that each person keep a record of goals and progress.
- Celebrate accomplishments.
- Praise individuals and teams.

C. Ask what skills they need to succeed.
- How can the group grow together?
- How can the group work together to solve problems by brainstorming?
- Incorporate continuous improvement. Work better, faster, smarter.
- Teach business rules, processes, and culture.
- Show how profit to the business turns into personal profit.
- Emphasize and model good communication.

D. As a manager, keep the big picture in mind and get it across to employees.
- Teach skills that transfer from the individual to the team and even to their personal lives.
- Promote profit for both individuals and the company.
- Stay aware of what's going on with people, processes, and profit.
- Always remember the big picture, post graphic reminders where they can be easily seen, and periodically review how this applies to each area of your department, as well as to the company as a whole.

E. Solve difficult issues as soon as they appear.
- Have participants work in pairs.
- Employ the underlying principles of the three sections of the meeting (asking what's going on, tracking goals, and determining needed skills).
- Have participants model what they would say and do by rehearsing how they will handle the problem.
- Give feedback and suggestions.

Please don't underestimate the importance of these meetings in helping you successfully lead a multicultural workforce. They may be applied to any workforce, but that discussion is beyond the scope of this book. Organize and conduct daily meetings as outlined in this chapter, and you soon will see the results: huge strides in capitalizing on your company's major capital—its people.

Before reading on, determine how you will implement daily meetings. When you do so, following the guidelines in this chapter, you will never look back.

Manager's Action Plan for Success

- Conduct a short daily meeting. This gets the day started with good communication and a clear understanding for everyone of what needs to be done.

- Become familiar with cultural holidays to ensure that they will not cause conflict with accomplishing the workload. If they do, come up with a solution.

- Find ways to make people feel comfortable and confident about themselves.

- Discuss how to solve work-related issues.

- Use numbers—dollars or quantity of goods produced—to measure a department's success.

- Bring inspiration to your team leaders by letting them read a motivational book in meetings.

- Take ideas from the meeting agenda template.

Chapter 14

How to Promote—or Fire—Multicultural Employees

Overview

This chapter discusses how best to promote employees in a multicultural workplace. For example, to begin with, the American system of promotion by merit must be explained to employees early on, because many other cultures promote only according to seniority or longevity with the company.

In addition, the chapter explains how best to handle the difficult issue of, when necessary, letting a member of your multicultural workforce go.

Promotion in America

One of the first points to understand about promotion and firing is that the rules may be different from culture to culture. For example, in the U.S., promotion is usually based on merit and ability. It is true that ability can increase with experience, and therefore someone who has been with the company longer may be a better bet for promotion. Nevertheless, in the end, the person receiving the promotion does so because the decision maker has determined that this employee can do a job better than the other candidates.

As the leader of a multicultural workforce, you should be aware that, in many other cultures, promotion by merit is not the case at all. In many Asian countries, for example, promotion is automatic and based on longevity: if you stay with the company for three to five years, you are moved up to supervisor, manager, or whatever is the next rung on the ladder. In addition, there likely are some cultures where you receive a promotion because you are the boss's friend or family member.

Therefore, during any new employee's initial orientation about the company, a non-native English speaker or immigrant in particular must be told how promotion works in your company. Let her know what it takes to get promoted. That way, she won't feel resentful when she sees someone receiving a promotion who has been with the company for a shorter time than she.

Of course you must never promise job candidates something that is not going to happen. If, on average, a promotion takes three or four years, say so. Tell them if they will get an annual review, as well as if a positive review will get them a raise and points that count toward promotion. From the beginning, inform them accurately of the policy in your organization.

Whom to Promote and When

Companies must be careful about whom they promote. While employees tend to feel that they should receive a promotion or at least a raise every year at the time of their review, in reality, promoting someone is a challenge: once you do so, you cannot put them back to where they were before, even if you learn that you made a mistake and they do poorly in the new position.

Understand that promotion is not for everyone. Some people would rather earn more money but without a change in rank, yet others want to get promoted more than anything and, if necessary, will even take a pay cut to do so. Others still want both a promotion and more money. There are all kinds of people in this world.

When considering someone for promotion, keep in mind that both technical and management skills are required. It is insufficient to be competent technically, because any kind of higher-level position will also require people skills and the ability to motivate a team to get production moving.

Never base your decision of whether or not to promote on your judgment alone. Solicit feedback from the person's supervisor and upper management, as well as from the employees who will report to the candidate should he or she receive the promotion.

When someone lets you know they are leaving the company and you are faced with filling their position, ask the employees in their work area whom they think would do best at being in charge. Ask them to evaluate the candidate using an evaluation form, and make sure the form covers such areas as language skills improvement, communication skills, leadership skills, and other pertinent qualities.

This research will help you avoid the mistake of promoting someone not yet ready for the responsibility of leading others. Remember that someone who is eager and intelligent but not respected by coworkers cannot be placed in charge of them. In addition, in a multicultural work-force they must be able to work with and motivate people of different cultures.

Sometimes employees may think that when they are friendly with the person making the promotion decision, they can get a free ride. Of course such a practice would render a workforce dysfunctional. When choosing whom to promote, look for those who motivate others and then be willing to invest generously in their training. Help them understand that they now will need to start thinking differently: they are no longer workers at the bottom of the ladder; they are supervisors. They will need to adopt a new perspective.

Promotion and Culture

When promoting someone to a supervisory position in a multicultural workforce, you must be particularly sensitive to the cultural aspect. It is usually a mistake to have everyone in a department or unit, including the supervisor, of the same culture—for example, all Chinese, Hispanic, Laotian, or whatever. The reason is that, in such a case, the unit members tend to isolate themselves from the rest of the team, which conflicts with what you are trying to accomplish: building a unified team composed of an entire workforce whose members combine and harmonize their strengths.

The best solution for such a case is to find someone from a culture close to that of the unit members; for example, in a unit of Chinese members, you might bring a Korean who has learned English as a second language. Just make sure that the Korean supervisor possesses excellent communication as well as technical skills, because he will need to interface with senior managers in addition to leading his unit.

After carefully selecting the right person to promote and giving him or her the promotion, it's time to celebrate the occasion. Make it joyous: treat the person well, take him or her out, throw a good party, and in general, make a big deal of it!

Do keep in mind that people may take the news of a promotion in different ways. For example, at a company where I worked, a production employee named Ming had come to the U.S. from China and completed an MBA program here while humbly continuing in his role as a factory worker. Ming performed many services, including translating when needed, and was consistently kind to those with whom he worked. For this reason, management decided to promote Ming to the position of supervisor, including doubling his salary.

Because we wanted to give Ming a happy surprise, we set up his new office without even telling him. A shy man, he was shocked when we told him he had been promoted and led him to his office. But he absorbed the news well. The only challenge he needed to overcome was setting aside his shyness in order to supervise a group of assertive women in his department, but with our encouragement and female assistants to help him, he succeeded well beyond expectations. He still is at the same company and very content.

In the U.S., the relationship between boss and employee is clear-cut— after work, you can be friends, but at work, it's strictly business. However, you need to be aware that in many cultures, it does not work that way: your boss is your boss for the rest of your life. This can pose a problem for someone taken from amongst her coworkers and promoted to be their supervisor overnight. Be sensitive to the fact that such a change is not easily dealt with by people of all cultures, and plan your actions accordingly.

Promoting Someone: The Nitty-Gritty

It is essential that you meet with the person you've decided to promote before the promotion takes effect. Sit down with him and explain clearly what the new job will entail and how it will differ from what he's been doing. When you announce to the individual's coworkers that he's receiving a promotion, explain clearly to them why this person was chosen, pointing out his leadership abilities and outstanding job performance.

Some people may think that once they've been promoted to a supervisory position, they no longer have to work, and in some cultures, this may be true. At a company where I worked, we once promoted a Vietnamese employee named Qua to supervise about 20 employees. Qua had been excellent at his former job and was gifted at overseeing and motivating the Vietnamese employees; however, we soon saw that Qua's promotion resulted in his becoming lazy. Had we not been so busy and failed to take the time to train Qua well, we might have averted what followed.

Qua began to use his work time to do things other than work when he was supposed to be working. Because he was so smart, it took us a while to figure out that he was disappearing during work time. Unfortunately, in the end we had to fire him. We lost not only a potentially great supervisor, but also a highly skilled and competent worker. But we learned a lesson.

One solution can be to instruct the new supervisor to remain in his area and work with the rest of the group he is now supervising. Suddenly giving someone a supervisory job without continuing any of his responsibilities for the job he did before can be confusing—he may not know what to do anymore. So make it clear that he is doing the same job as before but with the added responsibility of supervision.

Supervisors also may need to become more proficient in using the organization's computer systems. They have to be able to work unsupervised and evaluate their own job performance.

You may have to watch out for the occasional non-native English speaker who supervises others of the same culture and takes advantage of the fact that you don't understand their language. For example, I learned of one employee who had been promoted to supervisor but gave the best jobs only to his girlfriend. At first, no one in management knew that this employee was his girlfriend. The others in the area complained among themselves but didn't dare to tell senior management. In the end, the truth surfaced, and the supervisor was fired. But it was actually management that was at fault for failing to educate itself in the multicultural aspect of the situation—that some cultures customarily use position to gain advantage.

Promoting someone of another culture can be complicated. For example, the person may believe that now they are privileged: "Oh, I'm suddenly different from you," they may think in regard to their former coworkers. Such an attitude can be a problem.

When you promote people from a low level to a higher one, they may isolate themselves instead of asking for help when they need it. You can prevent this problem at the get-go by giving them plenty of training and mentoring: teach them how to speak to others, how to motivate those they're supervising, and develop them into a productive team.

On the plus side, by promoting people to be in charge of the same area where they've been working, you ensure that they're already familiar with how things work in that area. To further ensure their success, it's a good idea to use charts to track how the area improves following their promotion.

Once promoted, supervisors need training in various new skills. Provide training in how to conduct their own hiring interviews, for example, and how to select the best training program. They also need to know how to lay people off when necessary, to determine whom to fire and whom to retain, to conduct time and motion studies, to be effective in running their team, and many other skills.

Training workshops or seminars are easily available and highly recommended for employees promoted to the supervisory level with little or no supervisory experience. But even when such training is provided, it's no substitute for your working with and overseeing them at the job on a day-to-day basis. Don't skimp on mentoring. No matter how good they were at their previous job, don't expect them to be overnight experts in dealing with the people they're now supervising.

Learn how to spot the fairly usual common denominator for immigrants: an unwillingness to tell their manager if they're having trouble because they don't want to look weak. Talk with them often enough that they become comfortable talking with you, and then ask them matter-of-factly if anyone is giving them problems.

Sometimes a new supervisor might be having trouble supervising her friends due to over-familiarity or her friends taking advantage of her, in which case, you might need to transfer some of the friends to another department. Other times, trouble may come from people who harbor resentment that someone else was promoted instead of them; this situation also may require departmental changes.

Whom to Promote

Looking for the best people to promote is an ongoing task that's made easier by staying in direct daily contact with the workforce. You want to select those who not only earnestly try to finish their jobs on time but also encourage others, praising and assisting them when needed. Such behavior goes beyond job competence and evidences strong leadership abilities.

Watch your workforce members and learn to recognize the leaders. If you ask the people who work in the area whom they consider a good leader—discounting those who will recommend only their friends—they likely will choose someone who is helpful to others. Observe how well they communicate. Then combine this information with the numbers—their personal level of production—to arrive at a wise choice.

Letting Them Go

Letting people go is an unpleasant task that most managers would prefer to avoid, but sooner or later you will be faced with having to fire someone. You must handle this responsibility carefully, so as not to cause unnecessary rancor or send someone out the door disgruntled and vengeful.

Particularly with a multicultural workforce, it's essential to make sure that company rules are understood—and signed off on—from the beginning. By taking care of this during orientation, you avoid a situation down the road where someone claims he didn't know that employees were supposed to come to work on time, not steal from the company, not have a personal relationship with his employees, or whatever the offense.

Next, make sure that each time an employee breaks the rules by cheating with the time card, not coming to work on time, or whatever, this is discussed with the employee and documented with signatures from the employee's supervisor and you as manager.

After that you must follow through on doing what you said you would do. If you said you would fire them if they committed a certain offense, and they commit the offense anyway, you must fire them. Otherwise, no one will take you seriously.

The actual firing must be handled with care. Take the time to thoroughly explain why the person is being fired. Help him or her if you can, such as in finding another job. Consider that a misunderstanding could have occurred. Try to let the person leave with an attitude as positive as possible.

Keep in mind the cultural aspect to firing a member of a multicultural workforce. Understand that, particularly for immigrants, their reputation with their friends, family, and acquaintances is extremely important and will seem to be in jeopardy. Their mind will be racing: What will everyone think of me? Don't rub salt in the wound by insulting them. Keep the atmosphere as dignified and calm as possible and the topic on point, no matter what they did or how they behave now. Try to help them save face from any more embarrassment than necessary.

Key Lessons in Promoting Multicultural Employees

Lesson number 1: Make sure that new employees, particularly non-native English speakers, understand from the start what it takes to get promoted in your company.

Lesson number 2: Be extremely careful whom you select for promotion. They should be good at their job, possess excellent technical skills for the area they will supervise, and be skilled in communication and dealing with people. Pick leaders!

Lesson number 3: When you promote people in a multicultural work-force, keep them doing hands-on work as well as supervising. Don't let them mistakenly import the notion from another culture that they now don't have to work.

Lesson number 4: After promoting people, follow up by making sure they get the training they need in order to succeed. They'll need to polish their personal skills: how to greet people, make small talk, and communicate with the employees they now supervise, as well as with their fellow supervisors, managers, and upper management.

Lesson number 5: Make sure they understand their position as liaison between senior executives and the workforce and how to deal with this new responsibility.

Lesson number 6: Watch for difficulties that may arise as a result of the new supervisor having friends or family members working under his or her direction (for example, giving preferential treatment). If necessary, move the friend or family member to another department.

Manager's Action Plan for Success

- Explain promotion by the merit system to your new employees.

- Identify those in your department who, with additional training, might be candidates for promotion.

- Keep in mind that, to be promoted, the employee must be respected by coworkers.

- Provide promoted individuals with multicultural training at the managerial level.

- Pay attention to and carefully oversee newly promoted supervisors.

- Document employee behaviors that fail to meet company requirements. Having implemented this tool is necessary in the event of firing an employee.

Chapter 15

Everything Else to Help a Manager Succeed

Overview

This chapter includes points that don't warrant a chapter on their own, but need to be covered as valid aspects of successfully managing a multicultural workforce. Awareness of and proper dealing with these matters will take you still further toward becoming the best manager you can be.

Passion

Many immigrants come to this country because they possess great ambition. Often, it's the brave and intelligent individuals who leave their home country to seek their fortune abroad. When properly channeled, their ambition can become a passion.

If passion is not fed, it can fade. For this reason, immigrants often give up on their dreams and head back to where they came from. To get the most from the members of your multicultural workforce, nurture and encourage them. If the fire of ambition is no longer burning in them, take steps to bring that passion back.

In many of the U.S. companies where I worked, no one wanted to hear my ideas for how I best could fit in and take a leadership track, or how we might drive the company forward. I tried to express these ideas and clearly was ambitious, yet no one would consider me for a position higher than manager, and that was only after seven or so years of waiting, doing my best work, and hoping for a breakthrough. It was up to me alone to keep my ambition alive, and I felt frustrated.

Companies often promote people up the management ladder who never learn how to lead, motivate people, or listen. These companies need to start training their leaders to understand how to work with a multicultural workforce. These leaders have been put in charge of an incredible group of people who understand two or more cultures and bring invaluable experience, yet the treasure is going wasted. Leaders must learn that the more experience workforce members bring, the more creative they likely will become. The organization should benefit from this experience and creativity.

Talk with your workforce members and find out what they really want to do in the company. Discover their passion. Then take steps to direct them to work that will excite them and make them feel proud.

As you get to know your workforce members better, you'll see that many are doing a job other than what they feel passionate about. Never ignore this situation; address it with care. At the same time you help them understand the importance of their current job, help them set goals. Let them know exactly what it will take for them to move to the position they want. Give them an application form, and let them know that when that position becomes available, they will be considered for it. Familiarize them with the job requirements and help them with any necessary training.

Keep in mind that immigrants usually come to this country because they want to succeed, and they're eager to learn whatever is needed in order to bring this about. One step you can take to help your workforce members stay in touch with their passion is to make sure that they are always learning and developing their abilities. Let them take classes; provide a consultant, mentor, or coach; and suggest helpful books they can read. To remain a dynamic part of your workforce, its members need to feel that they are continually developing and improving their skills.

A good example was Shiong, a Vietnamese employee in one of the companies where I worked. Shiong was calm, a good communicator, and always kind to others. Management thought she was content in her manufacturing job until one day she announced to us, "I want to go to school," and then we realized that she was not satisfied.

We asked what she really wanted to do, and she answered, to our surprise, "I would like to work in finance or accounting." Usually a company has to hire someone with a high-level salary to do data entry, analysis, and problem solving, but our company was fortunate enough to have Shiong, who had already proven herself an excellent employee and expressed a passion to learn and apply these skills. This was a win-win opportunity.

Management encouraged Shiong to study her course of interest and transferred her to a job that developed her skills in data entry and information analysis. She glowed with happiness. Because she was following her passion, she worked and studied day and night without complaint, and often we witnessed her practicing her newfound skills. She analyzed our manufacturing process so that we knew exactly what problems it had, including how long each process took and what was needed to improve it.

She would do things like go up to someone and ask, "Why is this department so small? According to my data…."

Shiong became a much greater asset to the company than she ever would have been by staying in her manufacturing job. And because we had taken her from the workforce and trained her, she was willing to work for a much lower salary than someone already trained would have required. Everyone benefited.

Shiong went on to study accounting, which the company paid for. Eventually she was given a job in the accounting department, where she was a great success and saved the company considerable money. Her manufacturing background made her much more valuable than an accountant with a background only in accounting. Shiong understood company operations inside and out. She could pinpoint problems and find ways to increase efficiency. She also was easy for us to work with because of her familiarity with us and our operations.

You'll soon see that people tend to perform best when asked about their driving interests and ambition and then allowed to do what they really want. With immigrants and non-native English speakers, this subject needs special attention in order to overcome language problems or any culturally based reluctance to speak up and tell you what they really want to do.

Recognizing When Someone Needs Help

When you observe an employee frequently working late, coming in early, and not taking breaks, praise him for the excellent job he does but also ask if he needs help. People of many cultures don't like to admit when they need help, even if they're falling behind and suffering from overwork, because they're afraid someone else will take over their job. Offer them help in a way that does not make them feel threatened.

For example, you might tell them, "We'll just put an additional person here to help temporarily with the immediate overload. Let us know when you're caught up and don't need the help anymore. Then we'll reallocate the assistant." Make it clear why you're helping them, that the change is to their advantage, and that their job is not in jeopardy.

A smart young woman named Mai, from the Philippines, worked at one of the companies where I worked. Mai seemed to accomplish her tasks with the speed of a superhero, always finishing on time and with great quality, no matter how much work management gave her. Because she appeared to do this so easily, we kept giving her more and more work. What we didn't know was that Mai was working extra hours without telling us.

One day I found Mai at work on a Sunday at 5 p.m. "What are you doing here?" I asked her.

Mai finally couldn't suppress her resentment: "Look, none of you want me to have a personal life, right? That must be why you keep giving me more and more work."

"But that's because you keep finishing everything we give you," I answered, puzzled.

She looked at me and then lowered her eyes in shame. "To get all the work done, I must work extra hours behind the scenes that I never report to you."

With this information, management tracked Mai's work with a flow-chart, which made it clear why she'd needed to work so many hours to get the work done. We determined how much time her duties took and then spread the work over two departments, easing the load to a realistic amount. And we learned that, because of her cultural upbringing, she never would have said a word had I not found her working overtime. She believed she could not complain without risking her job.

In fact, I personally experienced such a situation. An immigrant working in the U.S. myself, I found that, in two years my workload with the company I worked for had doubled. I was working seven days a week and had become exhausted, yet I never complained for fear of being considered a troublemaker. In fact, in this new environment, I didn't even know how to complain.

No one ever asked me if I was having any problems. Management apparently took my lack of complaints as evidence that everything was fine. So the workload kept getting heavier and heavier, and it kept getting harder and harder for me to cope. Finally one night at 10 or 11 p.m., a manager found me still working and said, "Jinsoo, you need to go home. We need to find you an assistant."

Had I not been discovered working late that night, I would have continued what I was doing, working harder and harder with no one else realizing what I was doing. Worn out and frustrated, I would have grown increasingly resentful. But in the U.S., in this new kind of work world, I didn't know how to approach my seniors and ask for help.

The effective manager of a multicultural workforce will make it his business to see that the people working for him report how many hours they work, and if he finds them repeatedly working a lot of overtime, he'll identify the reason. Maybe they're having trouble with the computer system; maybe a personnel problem is to blame. Perhaps they need an assistant. Whatever the problem, take care of it.

Stress

In getting to know the members of your multicultural workforce, you will discover that many immigrants don't know how to handle the stress inherent in working in a new culture. What they do know is how to work hard; they don't want to have made all the sacrifices they made to come here and then lose their job. Frequently they continue to work past the point of exhaustion, until they're extremely stressed. Sometimes they're stressed from agreeing to take on a job they really aren't equipped to handle, but they try to do it anyway rather than ask for help in solving problems, fearful that doing so will make them look weak.

If employees work more than 10 hours' overtime per week, generally you should start sending them home on time for a while and then tell them to keep the overtime down in the future. At a company where I worked, management once learned that an employee, as a result of never taking time off to rest for fear of losing her job, had experienced two miscarriages. When we realized what was going on, we insisted she take an extended leave of absence so that she could go home, take care of herself, and have her baby. After she did that, she and the baby were fine, and she was ready to come back to work where her job was waiting, as we'd promised.

When, in observing the members of your multicultural workforce, you notice that an individual is behaving differently than usual—for example, acting uncharacteristically quiet or emotional—ask them what's causing them stress.

There are many ways to alleviate the stress felt by workforce members. Some companies provide gym facilities, massage therapists, and games or other stress-relieving activities because research has shown that such activities increase personnel's efficiency and, therefore, production. In some cases, you may need to move someone to a different job, adjust their workload, or find them an assistant.

131

While stress is a concern in any workforce, be sensitive to the aspects specific to immigrants and non-native English speakers. Because these individuals are burdened by an exaggerated fear of losing their job, they carry added stress. They also bring from their culture the notion that asking for help will make them look weak. Supervisors and managers may think these employees are doing well—after all, they're not complaining—and so give them more and more work. The already high stress level climbs higher and higher.

Consider Tin, who was Chinese. Tin had three children and a wife who became ill. In addition to his critical job in computer operations at the company where we worked, he had to take care of the children because his wife was unable to do so. Then his job started requiring more and more overtime. At home, the children woke him in the wee hours of the morning. The result: Tin was sleeping only two or three hours a night. However, he never mentioned this situation to anyone at work. In fact, he just kept smiling.

One day a coworker who had noticed that Tin was looking more and more exhausted finally asked him what was going on, and Tin told him. This coworker spoke to their manager and asked her to help Tin. The manager insisted that Tin go home to care for his family. Knowing how busy things were at work, Tin probably never would have asked for help on his own. He wanted to please his employers and feared losing his job, but he also wanted to take care of his family. Tin had stretched himself too far.

Eventually the company hired an assistant for Tin, and he taught her how to take over some of his load. By this time, though, the stress had taken its toll on Tin, who himself became so ill that he hardly was able to work. He was given a leave of absence, and after three months, finally recovered. Fortunately, the assistant he'd trained was able to cover for him. Tin's story serves as a great lesson in the importance of dealing with stress.

Humor

Humor can be a tricky subject in a multicultural workforce, but if you master it, it can become an effective tool. The key is making sure it's understood by all concerned.

A manager from a culture different from the employees he manages might think he said or did something really funny, only to look around and see that no one else is laughing, or that the few who are laughing look confused and are laughing just to please him. What members of one culture consider funny often is not looked at by members of another culture as anything funny at all.

There are two factors involved here. The first is simply language: non-native English speakers may not understand what their American manager is saying, including the nuances of the language that make what he said funny. The second factor is that people of different cultures don't always find the same thing humorous.

If members of one culture are laughing about something and those of other cultures don't understand the joke, the latter can feel left out, and this can create resentment. As a manager, it's up to you to be knowledgable and sensitive about this issue, because while humor may be a tricky subject, it's also one that can make a big difference in your workplace atmosphere, potentially contributing significantly to the workforce's team spirit and morale.

Humor can be a great stress reliever. You can use it as a beneficial tool in countless ways (for example, by treating a workplace incident with a humorous attitude, and sometimes even recording what happened or publishing a story about it in the company newsletter). Say that someone lightens the tension of a situation by saying something funny, and then everyone else laughs—make a record of it in a humor log. (**Note:** Only use "safe for work" pictures!) Encourage everyone to use their sense of humor. If they don't know how, teach them.

Part of the cultural training you provide for immigrants and non-native English speakers should be teaching them American humor. When you see that someone doesn't understand a joke, take the time to explain it to them. For members of a group to enjoy sharing humor, everyone in the group must understand.

On occasion, you might even go so far as to hire a comedian or humor coach to come to the workplace and teach your workforce members about simple humor. Pay attention to find out what kind of humor is working and what kind isn't. Assign someone the responsibility of keeping a log of the funny events that occur or that people say, placing photos or notes about these incidents in a scrapbook or on the bulletin board.

Make fun of what happens at work, but at the same time, be sensitive to which topics are considered humorous and which are not. Don't get upset if people sometimes don't laugh at your jokes. Remember that different cultures find different things to be funny. Learn about others' ideas of humor. Encourage everyone to familiarize themselves with the jokes and humor from other cultures. This practice will help greatly in breaking down any cultural barriers that may exist, as well as relieving workplace stress.

Humor may seem like a small matter, but use it and you'll see how a bit of humor can help the workforce develop into a more smoothly operating team.

A Balanced Life

Earning a living can become an all-consuming endeavor for immigrants in America. With a company primarily focused on production numbers, it can lose sight of matters such as the quality of an employee's family life. However, this should be a concern for the company as well, because giving all to the company can go on only so long before the stress becomes too much and the immigrant's job performance begins to suffer.

Production is important, but so is the employee's family. In addition to work, employees with school-age children are dealing with their kids' education in a culture where they haven't yet found their way. These employees need help, including time to find a proper school and ensure that their children get off to a good start.

Immigrants often come to this country with a big dream, and their passion to achieve that dream may make them try to accomplish too many things too fast. They may be working two jobs, going to night school, and also trying to work in a little time to enjoy themselves.

For example, I knew of a Mexican employee who worked as a mechanic but had dreams of seeing the whole U.S. He loved riding his motorcycle. Yet he worked a lot of overtime just to make enough money to live a decent lifestyle. He worked every Saturday.

Eventually, this employee quit his job, moved his things to a mobile home, and spent three months just traveling across the country. Then he returned and was rehired by the same company, this time as a much better employee. When someone has a dream, it usually works best to give them a leave of absence so that they don't have to quit; they can do what they want and then come back, feeling supported. After they return, they are 100 percent present, ready to become a company person and a member of a great team.

Due to unfamiliarity with their new country, people from other cultures often need extra time to deal with the non-work aspects of their lives, such as their children's schooling. They'll encounter problems that people born in this country don't have to face, and when that happens, let them tell you what the problems are so that you can help solve them. Counseling tends to help a great deal. This can be done by a supervisor or manager, or the company can hire a professional from outside.

You'll find that people new to the U.S. in your multicultural workforce have an initial lack of certainty about their new country and culture. They may not know what is expected of them or in what order to set priorities. Assisting them where needed in living a balanced life will give you an immensely valuable team member.

Flexibility in Difficult Times

If business is declining or the company is experiencing difficulty for any reason, it is always best to let the employees know. Use the open-book policy. Tell the workforce members why, for example, you need to lay people off and how long it will likely take to bring them back. In difficult times, everyone needs as much information as possible.

Your employees depend on their job security. If you need to lay someone off, help them as much as possible in finding a job elsewhere. If your company policy allows it, give them an excellent referral.

If it's the employee who is having a difficult time—for example, the woman who was going through a divorce and finding it hard to cope—let her know that she will still have a job if she leaves to deal with her problem. Otherwise, many immigrants would assume that you would not take them back.

If an employee is having personal difficulty and a slow production period is approaching, suggest that the employee take vacation at that time or work shorter hours than usual for a while. The employee can collect unemployment pay if he or she works only a few hours.

Finding Common Ground

A highly valuable tool in dealing with a multicultural workforce is finding common ground. All too often, it's the differences between various cultures that we stress. You can turn this around by instead emphasizing the similarities.

You'll soon see how far this approach takes a group of people from different cultures toward becoming a cohesive team. It can be especially effective in training programs where the goal is to familiarize people from different cultures with one another's culture. Begin by asking someone from one culture about some aspect of that culture, and then ask someone from a different culture how that aspect is similar in their culture. Watch how the two culturally diverse individuals start to become friends.

Manager's Action Plan for Success

- Identify methods for keeping employees passionate about their job.

- Help employees understand why their specific job is highly important to the company's operation.

- Assist employees in learning new skills.

- Identify ways for recognizing when an employee needs help.

- Alleviate job stress by utilizing gyms, massage therapists, and other stress-relieving programs.

- Encourage humor and laughter on the job.

- Allow employees the necessary time to handle family problems and emergencies.

- Keep employees informed about how the company is doing, not only in the good times but in the difficult times as well.

Chapter 16

Step-by-Step — Your Road to Success

Overview

A practical, step-by-step breakdown for any manager or human relations specialist in implementing the information in this book.

Using the Plan in This Book: Real Results

Several years ago, at the last company I worked for before starting my own business, I watched as amazing results followed the development of the program described in this book. By the end of my seven years with the company, we were experiencing phenomenal success.

Over time, my multicultural team members became highly Americanized. Instead of always eating fried rice, for example, periodically they began eating pizzas and hamburgers, and they especially loved American pies. They were drinking Coco Cola rather than tea all the time. They became adept at communication, with direct eye contact second nature. They loved celebrating American holidays, such as Thanksgiving with turkey and all the trimmings. They enjoyed celebrating the new year so much that they celebrated four: the Chinese, the lunar, the Southeast, and the American. They celebrated Hanukkah with a party; in fact, they were always happy for a reason to have a party.

They used the same skills at home that they learned at work, which helped their children adapt faster to living in America by improving their communication skills as well. At the same time, they revered their native tongue.

Each one became an ambassador for their own culture. They retained their pride in where they came from. They shared wisdom from the Talmud, Confucius, Allah, and so on. They brought such wisdom to the company.

They became comfortable with straightforwardly evaluating everyone involved in the work process, from the people who worked under them to themselves to their boss, and these evaluations greatly contributed to the company's success.

They no longer feared sharing their ideas with the company because they trusted the company not to ignore them. None of the company's products went to outlets because we produced almost zero damages. While other companies moved manufacturing overseas, ours stayed in San Francisco. Our exports to Europe multiplied. Our employees stayed with the company, resulting in a negligible turnover rate.

Most of those employees are still with the company today. They are its diamonds.

Try This Step-By-Step Plan to Start Motivating Employees

This chapter lists in sequence the steps that an HR manager, a manager of a multicultural workforce, or an executive in a multicultural company needs to take in order to implement the advice in this book. The result will be a multicultural workforce that becomes a real team, with the company gaining all the benefits that cultural diversity provides. Because every organization is different, these are general steps. Please adapt them to your own circumstances.

Survey

The first step you must take is to establish your company's health status with regard to multicultural matters. This is best accomplished with one or more surveys. Survey all levels of management to determine their attitude toward a multicultural workplace. Survey workforce members to determine their attitude toward cultural, ethnic, and language differences, as well as how well they think the company deals with these differences. Adapt the survey questions to your specific situation.

Hand out the survey at a company-wide meeting along with a suitable explanation. Follow up to make sure everyone answers all the questions on the survey and turns the survey in. Once all the completed surveys are collected, compile and analyze the results. Pass on these results to upper management so that any outstanding issues can be addressed. Repeat surveys every so often—say, two to four times per year—to provide yourself with an excellent progress index.

In addition to surveys, there are other ways to gather information on your organization's current health status regarding multicultural matters.

For example, you can use questionnaires, one-on-one interviews, or simply ask people during an informal conversation how they're doing and if they're happy. Supervisors may do this with people in their areas, whereas managers may talk with anyone in their department.

Bringing About Acceptance

Once you've established your organization's multicultural climate, your next step is to correct any negative attitudes regarding a multicultural workplace—particularly from upper management. A negative attitude at the top of a company will make creating a cohesive multicultural team impossible. If such an attitude exists at your company and you cannot change it—and if your ambition is to succeed at motivating a multicultural workforce—you might as well look for work elsewhere. To create a climate where cultural diversity is regarded positively and with understanding, you need upper management's cooperation and support.

To help upper management develop awareness of the benefits of a multicultural workforce, begin by giving them a copy of this book. Talk with them one on one, explaining how a thriving multicultural workforce contributes more than satisfaction of a legal requirement or moral duty. Point out the range of skills that multicultural workforce members bring. Go over the positive points covered in this book's earlier chapters.

When it's middle managers or supervisors who aren't keen on leading a multicultural workforce, follow the same advice as for upper management. Discuss their objections and educate them about the benefits of employing a multicultural workforce. Make it clear that these benefits far outweigh apparent drawbacks.

Policy Formulation and Implementation

Once upper management has "seen the light" regarding employing a multicultural workforce, your next step is to review company policy and make any needed changes to ensure further acceptance and success for this workforce. Review policy on hiring and firing, including details such as accommodating multicultural holidays, providing adequate ESL and other needed training, and the various additional factors outlined in this book. Include in policy changes details about how employees are to be praised and rewarded for outstanding performance, for example, with promotion.

Clarify in orientation materials that this policy is for the benefit of the company as a whole, not just added benefits for non-native English speakers. The workplace harmony and increased production that result from this policy will help everyone see its value.

Once the revised company policy is written, post it on the notice board for everyone to see. Make sure that it clearly expresses the company's current attitude toward multiculturalism (for example, "We respect people of all cultures and do not discriminate on the basis of culture," and so on). In addition, you might have cards printed that express this policy, which employees can carry around as reminders that the company is open to all cultures.

Managers should meet to determine how best to implement the new policy. Generally, one person is chosen to be in charge. This should be someone who fully understands the issue—ideally, a successful immigrant or someone with a non-U.S. background. Such an individual will bring a solid subjective perspective of the challenges and benefits inherent in employing a multicultural workforce. This person also must be loyal to the company, having proved that they have its success at heart. In the case of a larger organization, one person from each culture might be chosen to take charge of implementing the policy for that particular ethnic group.

In my experience, I've found it sufficient to designate one person in charge of a company's multicultural issues. This person becomes the organization's expert on such issues. They must be trained both initially and on an ongoing basis in order to stay abreast of any developments.

Each department head should then meet with his or her department to determine how to handle issues specific to that department.

Training

When making organizational changes for developing a successful multicultural team, remember that training is vital. Reading this book is just the first step.

To begin with, the company's CEO and upper management must be trained on the issue of optimally developing a multicultural workforce. Then managers must be trained on how to motivate employees in such a workplace. Then, supervisors.

Once the company's leaders have read this book, bring in outside instructors, seminar leaders, and coaches, or conduct the training yourself.

The gist of this training should be how to motivate people of different cultures, how to get them to work together creatively in harmony, and at the same time, increase efficiency and productivity. Be sure to provide instruction on how to implement current company policy on multicultural issues including hiring, firing, meetings, rewards, and the like.

Make sure everyone understands that this training is not just a one-time affair. People are human and need to be reminded. In the same way that many companies hold an employee safety meeting or training session once every quarter or so, so should a company hold a training session on multicultural issues. Such a session should include a review of progress in implementing the new policy on multicultural issues (for example, by asking if people from cultures outside the U.S. believe that they are being treated fairly). These training sessions, run by the individual in charge of multicultural issues, will serve as preventive measures for handling small matters before they turn into large ones.

Meetings

The next step is to institute meetings as covered in Chapter 13 of this book. This includes monthly meetings company-wide, as well as daily meetings between managers and the supervisors who report to them and between supervisors and the employees they supervise. Meeting leaders must ensure that all attendees leave with an understanding not only of immediate goals and production issues but also of how the company is doing and what direction it's taking.

Resources

Make videos, CDs, books, magazines, and online resources with information about various cultures available to employees who want to learn more. Prominently display these resources.

Also make sure that employees know to whom they can turn if they're experiencing cultural issues that they need to discuss. The person who counsels them should keep a record of the issue and its outcome, as well as ask the employee to sign the document indicating whether or not they're happy with the resolution; if not, an appointment should be scheduled to talk about the matter further. Clearly, the individual you entrust to counsel others should be empathetic as well as highly professional. If you take on this responsibility yourself, hold yourself to the highest standard.

For Multicultural Success on the Job, Begin Today!

Now it's *your* turn to start *your* action plan! As you do so, watch the members of your multicultural staff grow more and more open-minded. See how they begin to trust you, enjoy camaraderie with one another—*and improve that bottom line.*

Bonus Section

How to Hire the Best Multicultural Employees

Overview

The Bonus Section delves deeply into issues you'll likely encounter when hiring employees who speak English as a second language. For example, what's wrong with the current application forms? How much does interviewing applicants from a culture outside the U.S. differ from interviewing others? All aspects of hiring are covered so that you as a manager or HR professional can make the right decisions.

Once a new employee is hired, you need to know how to get them started so that they succeed in the company, positively contributing to your great team and enhancing their own life as well. The Bonus Section covers this issue.

Avoid Stereotyping

Unfortunately, the practice of stereotyping others abounds in the workplace as well as outside it. For example, many people say that individuals from India excel at information technology (IT). Or they say that the Chinese work best in manufacturing. They may say that Hispanics should work in the construction field. Or whatever.

Thinking this way is absolutely the wrong approach to hiring any kind of workforce.

What I found successful was remaining open-minded to people from any culture (including the American culture!). I cultivated a willingness to hire those with different experiential and cultural backgrounds, while at the same time looking for the best people I could find for company positions that needed to be filled.

I have learned to be very broad-minded. In over 20 years' experience of hiring and managing employees, I witnessed many people develop into comparative geniuses who began with no background or education in the area that became their specialty. I learned to believe that anyone can be educated or trained in the particular field to which they're drawn.

I am my own example. At the university I attended in Korea, I majored in engineering and manufacturing. I obtained my master's degree and initial work experience in that field. Now, however, my job consists of training and motivating others, consulting, and public speaking. Over the years I've come to strongly believe that anyone can do anything that they make up their minds to do.

When hiring employees, while I looked for successful experience in an area similar to the one where we had an opening, those two areas did not have to be identical. For example, I might hire someone to work in manufacturing whose previous experience included successfully selling vegetables at a market in their country of origin.

The hiring process is complex. You must follow equal opportunity regulations. You can ask certain questions in interviews but not others. Because it is so difficult to fire an employee once he's been hired, you must be extremely careful to hire the right person to begin with.

Many companies follow equal opportunity laws only because they have no other choice. They feel forced to hire people from unfamiliar ethnic and religious backgrounds and resent this necessity, but this feeling is shortsighted. The most effective hiring practice is to find the best person for an open position, at the same time taking advantage of the diverse educational and experiential background of an applicant from a different culture.

Think of it: Your source for hiring new employees is the whole world. Look for the best individuals without regard to culture or religion and then make the most of the diverse skills and talents that different cultures produce.

Finding People from Diverse Cultures

Once you have committed to bringing people of diverse cultures into your workplace, the next step is finding the people you want.

At the company where I worked, we placed job ads in the local Chinese, Indian, Vietnamese, Hispanic, and other newspapers, along with the ads placed in mainstream American newspapers. We also used Craig's List, Monster.com, and other similar Web sites. Generally, we placed the ads in English, because we wanted to hire people who could at least read English.

We were careful to make clear in our ads what we had to offer and what we needed in return so that people who responded to the ad knew what to expect. We provided information briefly describing our company, what positions we wanted to fill, and so on. We stated that we were looking for people with related experience in their country of origin. We told them they should be able to speak at least some English and be prepared to work with people of many cultures.

Our job ads produced a lot of responses. Because we did not provide our phone number in the ads, applicants had to respond with a letter by either postal mail or e-mail. These written responses gave us our first clue to their English skill level. Then we wrote back to them and asked about their English-speaking ability. This correspondence often gave us an idea of their nationality—something we could not have asked about in an interview—however, what we were really looking for were their skills and accomplishments.

If we were looking for a supervisor, for example, we wanted someone with at least some management experience in their country of origin. Perhaps they had run a small retail store or the like. We also looked for signs to tell us if they were team players and good at working with others.

Multicultural Hiring in America—The Basic Flaw

In the U.S., people from other countries usually are hired based on what they have done since arriving on American soil—what courses they've taken, what jobs they've held, and so on. But this focus completely misses out on the real picture of what the person has to offer. It makes hiring those from other countries a risky—and often losing—proposition. Yet I've seen this basic mistake made repeatedly by managers, HR professionals, and others hiring multicultural employees in this country.

I'm not saying that you don't want to know what the job applicant has done since coming to the U.S. I'm saying that their most pertinent education and job experience are what they did in their country of origin. For example, what school did they graduate from there? What university degree they did they obtain, if any? For what company did they work, at what position, and how successful were they? This background information will complete the picture you need to make your hiring decision. Obtaining it may require some research but is worth the effort.

Ask employees at your company whose country of origin is the same as that of the job applicant about the school and university that the applicant graduated from; this will give you an idea of the quality of the applicant's education. Also ask about the companies where the applicant worked. Extend your research to the Internet. This not only gives you a good idea of the applicant's background but also gives a candidate you want to impress a favorable idea of you and your company. Your time will be well spent.

Hiring people who lived and worked in countries outside the U.S. can bring skills to your company that otherwise it might not obtain. For example, my university major in textiles cannot be found in the U.S.—or in Korea, now, as well—because it's considered a dead industry. However, there are countries, such as some in Latin America, where this is not the case; people are still being trained in textiles. And this training can be useful in the proper environment in the U.S today.

When I was looking for a job in the U.S. that required manufacturing experience similar to mine, I found a good match with a company that made belts. While I had no experience working with leather, upper management was flexible enough to recognize my skills and hire me. As it turned out, my training and experience were invaluable to their operations.

The Application Form

All too often, U.S. companies use job application forms with the same basic flaw discussed in the preceding section: they ask immigrants for background information beginning with their arrival in this country. As noted, this is a mistake.

The first job or jobs an immigrant took right after coming to the U.S. are barely relevant, because nearly every person in this situation takes any job they can get, just to get a foothold in this country. What is important is how the individual developed the opportunity—the results they obtained. You should be aware that it's not unusual to find a highly educated person who was, for example, a doctor or engineer in their country of origin, driving a cab in the U.S. just to get started.

The application form should include sections where an applicant can list and elaborate on their background experience in their country of origin, including names of schools and places of higher education, companies worked for with contact information for verification of references, and so on. The form should make it clear that their non-U.S. background will be treated exactly the same as that of an applicant from the U.S.

It is vital that you check references. If an applicant says they went to a certain college in their country of origin, check with that college to make sure they really did. Ask for a copy of their diploma from the school where they claim to have graduated. Keep in mind that anyone can buy a fake diploma, including in the U.S., with no study required. Or sometimes people may say that they went to college in the U.S. when in fact it was an ESL program. So check references diligently. Speak with people who knew the applicant in the past. And make sure that an applicant's papers are in order so that you can verify that they are legally permitted to work in this country—this is essential.

It's not that you want to distrust applicants; it's just that you must protect your company from making mistakes that are hard to correct. Simply verify the information an applicant gives you, using the Internet and e-mail to make your task quicker and easier than it would have been in the past. If in this process you find that an applicant has deliberately falsified information on his or her résumé or application form, *do not hire that applicant.*

Also keep in mind that, in examining references, you may have to read between the lines. Frequently, people who agree to serve as references say a lot of flattering things and gloss over any problems. You may need to phrase questions cleverly to get the information you're after. When speaking to the person serving as reference, in addition to asking if the applicant was good at their job, also ask, for example, how many people they supervised, what percent of the time they were absent, why they left, and so on. On their résumé, the applicant may have left out the information of why they left their previous employment, but you may find out that they were fired. In that case, of course, you'll need to know why. Find out if they learned lessons they can apply to a job with your company.

Often the résumé itself is not relevant, because many people who come to the U.S. from other countries don't know how to write a standard résumé, and this will become apparent during an interview. If possible, you'll want to have applicants interviewed by someone of the same culture. Such a person likely will be familiar with the schools and companies listed by the applicant on the application form and can verify their credibility.

That Vital First Interview—What to Look for and What to Say

The first interview is key, particularly with members of a multicultural workforce. Not only what you ask, but also what you tell the applicant about your company, are vital in establishing a clear understanding between you. Ten years after my first interview at a company where I worked, I still remember exactly what was said. Much employment trouble arises from an initial misunderstanding on the part of the employee resulting from insufficient information provided by the employer at the first interview. Such a misunderstanding leads to expectations that do not match reality.

Remember in hiring that it's the individual you will be bringing into the company, not an application form. Use the form as a stepping-off point, but look at the individual, ask them questions, get a sense of whether they are being honest with you. Look for straightforwardness—if you ask whether they have experience with a certain task and they say, "No, but I can learn," give them credit for confidence and honesty. Look for people who show interest in the company, who are positive and eager to be part of your team, and who want to contribute to the company's success.

Never ask such questions as what is your family background or are you single or married. Even asking where they come from is inappropriate. Be straightforward yourself—tell them about your company's history and what it's doing today, giving them an accurate picture of the organization they're considering joining.

Don't try to make the picture deceivingly rosy. If your company does manufacturing, and employees are expected to work eight hours from 8 to noon and from 1 to 5, Monday through Friday, with one hour for lunch and one 15-minute break, say so. If you require that everyone arrive on time in the morning, tell them. If you have a probation period preceding granting benefits, let them know. If benefits include one week's paid vacation and one week's unpaid vacation per year, a 401k plan, and paid medical insurance for employees but not their families, lay this all on the table.

Your straightforwardness with individuals who often are uncertain about so many things in a new country will help them and will show your sincerity and kindness. In this same vein, let them know that it's okay to make mistakes, that they will be part of a team and free to ask questions, that they can make suggestions, and so on. Make their job responsibilities clear, as well as the opportunities you'll give them for learning and elevating their position. Take care that everything you say is factual.

Tell applicants about your company's policy regarding people from cultures outside the U.S. so that they can get a feel for how they can move up. For example, you might say, "We have managers from Mexico, China, and other places who were lacking English skills when they started working here, but we saw their potential and how hard they worked. We provided them with the opportunity to become managers with extra coaching and training, and they took advantage of the opportunity. Our investment paid off all around." Let applicants see that there's hope for them to grow in the company too. Just make sure that what you say accurately reflects reality—any misrepresentation of the situation would bring trouble later on.

At least one company I know of uses this successful interview strategy: Applicants participate in three separate interviews from three different people. The first interview is with a supervisor or manager over the area where the applicant would be working, ideally someone from their own culture. The second and third interviews are with two managers, two executives, or a manager and an HR professional, respectively. Considering how expensive it is to hire someone, as well as how difficult it is to fire them if you make a hiring mistake, it's worth every bit of extra care you take in the hiring process to make sure you've found the right person.

Points to Watch for in the Selection Process

One of the first warning signs you must watch for in a job applicant is dishonesty. If you find that someone has lied to you or given you a false picture of their education, work experience, or the like, don't hire them.

Lack of confidence is another negative characteristic. Even if someone is not highly experienced, you want a positive, can-do attitude.

Beware of those who arrive at a job interview looking sloppy, unkempt, or even dirty. A neat, clean, well-groomed appearance evidences personal pride that will be reflected in job performance.

At the same time, allow yourself a little flexibility. I once hired a man who arrived at the job interview smelling of fish, and he turned out to be one of the best employees I ever hired. He was an immigrant who had taken any job he could get in this country—working in a fish market—in order to support his family, and he came to the interview during his lunch break. I saw his positive qualities during the interview, so I hired him despite the smell. Once he started working for the company, the smell of fish disappeared, but his positive qualities remained and grew.

Pay attention to education and job experience an applicant brings from their country of origin. Value and take advantage of these assets as an added contribution to your company.

Notice if an applicant shows difficulty in elaborating on their background due to language limitations, and try to make it easier for them to do so. If you've done some research on their country, you'll be equipped to ask questions, show an interest, and listen attentively. Offer them coffee; don't act rushed. Help them relax. Be patient.

Beware of unrealistic expectations toward your company ("Oh, I want to be the CEO"). Unrealistic expectations will lead to disappointment and dissatisfaction, leading to problems for you down the road.

At the same time, value healthy ambition. Consider the example of Julie, who was Cambodian. Julie's ambition was to get educated, and she made this clear during her hiring interview. She was a polite individual who smiled often and had a mild temperament, yet she was also very strong. I found out during the interview that she had come to this country on a fishing boat after surviving six years of living in a refugee camp. I knew there was something special about a woman who still could smile after the experiences Julie had gone through, so I hired her, even though she could barely speak English.

Julie made it clear upfront that she preferred not to work overtime because she wanted to have time to pursue her ambition of earning a master's degree. Though I was unsure if she would leave the company after completing her education, I took the risk. I even assigned assistants to help with her job when she couldn't be there. After two years, the risk paid off. Julie graduated, moved on to upper management, and is still with the company. The last time I saw her, she was still smiling. Her ambition benefited the company as well as Julie.

When asking why an applicant left his or her last job, watch out for a critical attitude toward a previous employer. Keep in mind that one day they might be saying the same things about you.

Watch for unrealistic pay expectations, and let the applicant know upfront. Never hire anyone based on false presumptions. Otherwise, there's no question that the backfire will come; it's just a question of when.

If an applicant shows intolerance toward people with a religion different from theirs, don't hire this person. I've actually seen managers try to pressure people working under them to become a Christian or a

Buddhist. Curb such a disaster in the making. Tell the applicant that your company policy includes not pushing any religion on anybody.

Also make clear in advance to your applicant that sexual harassment is unacceptable and once discovered will result in job loss. Emphasize this point especially when considering a candidate as manager who would have authority over many employees of the opposite sex. Be aware that in some cultures, for example, it's OK for a man to treat women as inferior.

Determine the individual's ability to communicate in your workplace with basic language and communication skills tests, and evaluate their performance on these tests. Make sure that they'll be able to read sufficient English to understand your memos, the company policy handbook, and so on. They should also be able to write English well enough to carry out the functions of the particular position for which you're considering hiring them.

If yours is a manufacturing environment where employees need to be able to count and make mathematical calculations, test and evaluate their performance on these areas as well as English. Let them know in advance that this is part of the hiring process and then administer simple but formal tests in these and any other skills needed for the position in question. Make sure that their test performance indicates they can handle the job for which they're applying.

There are cases in which you'll want to take on someone with weak skills in one area in order to gain their strong skills in another area. For example, if someone is a highly qualified engineer with weak English skills but committed to improving their English, you can hire them and provide them with English lessons. However, if the open position requires that they supervise others, they should be able to read and write English fairly well from the start.

Don't automatically discount an applicant who speaks English poorly during the job interview. Be aware that many non-native English speakers read and write English quite well although their spoken English may be poor, perhaps because their English classes did not focus on conversation. Consider whether or not their language skills are adequate for the job you're seeking to fill, and balance this information with other strengths or weaknesses the individual may bring.

Getting a New Employee Off to a Good Start

It takes time, effort, and expense to hire good people. Once you hire a new employee, you want to make sure that they stay.

The first month is especially important for nurturing a new employee. It's been found that most people who quit a new job do so within the first three weeks; if they stay longer, chances are that they won't quit. Once they've been there a month, you can start to breathe easier. By this time, they've begun to feel like part of the "family." But those first few weeks are crucial.

Make sure that the probationary period is sufficient for them to prove themselves, but not so long that they feel distrusted past the point where they've shown what they can do. And don't forget that this time period is for their benefit as well—it gives them time to evaluate whether or not they like working for you.

Make a point every single day of talking to the new hire and getting her feedback before she leaves for the day. Ask her how things went. An HR professional should also periodically spend time with a new employee. In the beginning, expect the new hire to feel uncomfortable: after all, she's dealing with new people in a new environment. If she spent 10 years at her former company, everything new may feel wrong. So don't let yourself be too busy or forget to check in with the new employee before she leaves for the day. Do all you can to spare the company the expense of her quitting, and yourself the trouble of having to start the hiring process all over again.

At one company where I worked, an American named Liz was hired as a supervisor. Liz brought previous experience working in a multicultural environment, but most of the people she'd worked with were Hispanic. Because she spoke some Spanish, she'd felt close to them. The employees in our workforce, however, were predominantly Asian.

Liz came with the preconceived notion that the Asian members of our workforce spoke only Chinese, Vietnamese, or Korean, and since she didn't know any Asian languages, she was at a loss as to how to communicate with them. Also, she didn't know that Asians generally don't directly say what they're thinking. So there was a terrible problem with miscommunication between Liz and the people she was supposed to supervise. In fact, she thought they were ignoring her.

If only we had implemented our daily meetings before Liz left in frustration, she would have learned that her impression of being ignored by the employees she supervised was a misconception. We could have brought her together with the other supervisors and resolved the issue. But we thought we didn't have time—that we were too busy.

Losing Liz was major for the company, because she was an expert in the area where we'd placed her. But it got our attention, and we realized that we should have spent more time with her when she arrived. It's not unusual for a company to see its mistakes in hindsight.

At the same company, we hired a Korean American woman who was extremely quiet. We placed a great deal of trust in this woman, but one day someone mentioned to a manager, "She spends a lot of time sending personal e-mails."

Management checked into this and found out it was true, so we gave her a warning—but she kept sending the personal e-mails. Finally we discovered that she had another job on the weekends, and she also was going to school. We saw nothing wrong with this, and in fact we admired her ambition and motivation, but we didn't want to pay her to finish her homework during the time when she was supposed to be working for us. We realized that she felt too pressured from trying to do more than she could handle, so after six months we had to let her go.

Had our orientation program explicitly spelled out what was acceptable and what was not, perhaps this employee would have behaved differently. Perhaps in another country, what she did would have been viewed as okay. We had trusted her with a lot of freedom; maybe she thought, "This company makes a lot of money, and they won't care." But we should have looked for warning signs in the initial interview and sorted out what was most important to her before we hired her. Straightforwardness is the best way on both sides. Dishonesty inevitably leads to getting caught.

In this case, we made the mistake of hiring someone who was too ambitious for the job we had to fill. We should have made it clear to her from the beginning exactly what we expected, what our rules were, and what was not acceptable. And had we talked with her every day to see how she was doing, we might have noticed sooner what was wrong. It's not a matter of intimidating, appearing threatening, or instilling fear—quite the contrary. It's a matter of hiring carefully, making boundaries and expectations clear, and helping the new employee to excel at the job.

More Pointers for Managers and HR Professionals

Managers and HR professionals responsible for hiring—and, particularly, interviewing—job applicants in a multicultural workplace need special training for this task. Such training should include exposure to the various cultures with which hiring personnel will be dealing.

I once asked a female job candidate from China about her background in her home country and received the answer, "I was an engineer." Because of my Asian experience, I understood that when a person from China says they were an engineer, it likely means they were a technician; I've found this a common point of mistranslation. I don't believe that the woman was being deliberately dishonest; however, the information she provided was incorrect and, without my familiarity with the Chinese, could have led to a wrong hiring decision.

Because applicants often do exaggerate their qualifications in a job interview—while understating any troubling issues—some skepticism on the part of the interviewer is understandable. One applicant told me, "Oh yes, I managed a huge workforce at a top company. I had a great many responsibilities," and I thought to myself, "Right! You probably were a supervisor." But research revealed that this man oversaw more than 1,000 employees in a company of 10,000. He wasn't exaggerating at all. So while you must keep an eye out for trouble, you still must keep an open mind.

Another applicant told me he had worked as a bank executive in his home country. When I asked why he was applying for a job that paid only $30,000, he replied it was because he was new in this country and needed to start somewhere. His résumé was amazing. You may find immigrants with extensive, valuable experience from their country of origin who don't know how to present their accomplishments so therefore understate them. Still, overstating is more common than understating.

Remember the importance of familiarizing yourself with education standards, companies, and work practices in other countries. Learn how the systems work: basic education, university, corporate, and so on. In many countries, for example, staying at a company for three years results in an automatic promotion, and another promotion after three more years. This happens without regard to job performance or merit. In the U.S., however, we recognize that we need to promote people to management who exhibit true leadership qualities. We give them challenging tasks with which to prove themselves.

The best way to learn about the various practices in different cultures—and become proficient at hiring individuals from those cultures—is to talk with their people. Develop contacts. Then supplement your self-education with Internet research.

You'll find out that in Asia, the high school and university a person attended are considered highly important, and that different schools are known for different qualities.

If you verify that an applicant worked at one company for many years, this may not show their value at the company, but at least you'll know they're stable. While in the U.S. people who change companies every five years or so are considered highly valuable and motivated toward success, in Asia, it's essential to work for one company throughout one's life. Hiring personnel need to understand such national differences.

Unless you are interviewing for a position involving speaking with customers, don't judge applicants from outside the U.S. by their English. You could have a diamond sitting across from you but reject them because of a problem that could easily be fixed. Listen well; allow a translator if needed. I've hired many individuals whose English was poor but who turned out to be extremely valuable to the company.

Phat is an example. He was from Thailand, and was really funny and eccentric guy. His English was so poor that, when I first interviewed him, he couldn't communicate anything about himself or his background. I couldn't even find out if he had graduated from high school. But I recognized his humor and engaging personality.

I needed a driver for the company where I worked. Phat showed me his driver's license, so I hired him as a delivery truck driver and carefully monitored his progress. He loved talking to people, and when they couldn't understand him, he used hand signals, always joking and making people laugh. I decided he was worth a time investment, so I spent a lot time talking with him and helping him with his English.

Over time, Phat's English improved greatly. His personality became more and more evident, and I saw that he was highly responsible. He was promoted to supervisor of transport and doubled his original salary. Later, he became a senior manager. All his special qualities became the company's assets.

Sometimes in job interviews, applicants from countries outside the U.S. make small language errors that result in confusion. One job candidate stated to me that in his home country he had worked as a salesman.

When I asked what product he sold, he replied, "Drugs." After listening to his description of his job activities and hearing him use the word "dealing," I became convinced that he was a drug dealer. But it turned out that he simply didn't know the word for "pharmaceuticals." The man had been a pharmacist.

Such errors are common. Many immigrants mix up the words "chicken" and "kitchen." "I used to work in a chicken," they may say. One day at church shortly after arriving in this country, a church member asked me about my religious heritage, and I said I was a "prostitute." I meant to say "protestant."

The moral of such humorous stories is don't jump to conclusions. Ask more questions until you get to the truth.

Not all hiring stories are funny or end happily. A company where I worked had a new Laotian employee who soon began stealing from the company. Before we ever hired him, we should have seen from his eyes, which were filled with anger, that something wasn't right. It's important that hiring personnel recognize emotionally destructive people and not hire them. He was new to this country and had no references, but we tried to be kind and took him on anyway—a mistake. Always insist on references, even if they refer to contacts in the person's home country.

By hiring carefully and managing intelligently, you'll wind up with a strong multicultural workforce, including many gems that will make a long-term, positive difference to your company. Be sure to provide new employees with a comprehensive orientation program that lets them know what to expect, and ask that they sign a form indicating they understand. Give them all the training they need to excel at their job. Keep communication lines open and address any issues as they arise. Encourage humor and camaraderie in the workplace. Reward people generously for a job well done.

Final Words

The successful manager of a multicultural workforce recognizes that workplace procedures are different when dealing with cultures from outside the U.S. It's essential to respect other cultures. If you hire a Muslim, be aware that they will be bowing toward Mecca at certain times during the day. Respect this practice and allow for it.

Some cultures frown on men and women working together, yet your workplace may require that they do so. If you've done your cultural research before interviewing a job candidate, you'll be aware of such issues and prepared to talk about them. The candidate may want to wear a veil or a turban during work, and you likely will have no problem with that. Just be sure that both you and the candidate understand one another's requirements before a hiring decision is made so that the decision won't be a mistake for either side.

Managing a multicultural workforce includes all the elements present in managing any workforce—and more. The result of making the effort to do this right will be a great multicultural team representing the best of all the cultures from which your workforce is built.

About the Author

Jinsoo Terry is the founder and CEO of Advanced Global Connections, LLC, a company she formed in 2004 to meet the demand for training, consultancy, and other services related to multicultural business activities in the U.S. and abroad. She is a well-known columnist and speaker in the U.S., in Asia, and increasingly in Europe and has gained a reputation as an expert on multicultural and motivational issues. In Korea, she has become well known and signed her first book contract with one of the country's top publishers.

Born in Korea in 1956, Jinsoo broke with gender tradition in her country by studying for and gaining a master's degree in engineering and, after graduating from Pusan National University in 1981, capturing a leading job as an engineer and manager of the R&D department in Ilshin Corporation, Korea—customarily a man's job in a man's world.

Jinsoo has a taste for challenges and winning. She decided to emigrate to the U.S., where she made her way up the success ladder despite her initial limited English proficiency. Although she possessed an engineering degree, in 1985 she began working as a lead assembler at Nellcor, a Hayward, California, medical equipment manufacturer. Between 1987 and 1993, she worked as production supervisor at Circa Corporation. She then joined Cut Loose, the company where she worked from 1993 to 2005, starting as production manager and moving to director of manufacturing and eventually vice president of manufacturing.

Jinsoo's increasing skills in managing the widely multicultural workforces at the companies where she was employed eventually led to the demand for her to train Korean managers in how to do business in the U.S., as well as to speak at international events on the subject and assist the U.S. Department of Commerce with multicultural trade issues.

Always enthusiastic about helping other immigrants experience an easier transition than she did, Jinsoo has been involved in many initiatives to help those for whom English is a second language and who are struggling to succeed in the U.S. She cofounded the Greater Hispanic Chamber of Commerce in San Jose, California, and remains active in that organization. She also cofounded Success Builders International in Silicon Valley to help train business owners and professionals in communication, leadership, and human relations. As a result of her own enormous benefits from membership in a Toastmasters speaking club, in 1998 she founded a San Francisco chapter, calling it the Rhino Business Club (for the thick-skinned animals that charge straight ahead), where she has mentored more than 800 young businesspeople in public speaking and leadership.

In 2006, SBS TV in Korea featured Jinsoo in a documentary on F.U.N. management viewed by an audience of an estimated two to three million people. Following the program, Jinsoo received book offers from 20 publishing companies, including Random House Korea, and signed a contract with Kim Young Sa, one of Korea's top three publishers.

Having overcome her own cultural and language barriers to success, Jinsoo is well known in U.S. business circles. A member of the National Speakers Association, she makes frequent speeches and presentations at major events and conferences. She is a columnist for *The Korea Times*, America's largest Korean newspaper, as well as for the *Korean Christian Times* and www.younwoo_forum.com, a favorite Internet destination among Korean businesspeople. *The Korea Times* voted her Most Influential Korean American, she was featured on CBS *Eyewitness News* in the San Francisco Bay area, and ABC TV hailed her as one of the top 10 Asian Pacific Island community leaders.

San Francisco Mayor Willie Brown proclaimed July 10, 2001, "Jinsoo Terry Day" in recognition of her contributions to the San Francisco business community, including founding the Rhino Business Club to help the city's businesspeople with both business and self-development, bringing together the various Pacific Rim countries to enhance business opportunities for the San Francisco business community, and helping the city's business community to build global connections. Jinsoo also was proclaimed Minority Business Advocate of the Year in 2003 by the U.S. Department of Commerce and had been runner-up in 2002. In 2003, she was awarded a certificate of appreciation for her assistance with minority outreach and trade promotion activities, and in 2004, she received the U.S. Commercial Service Export Award.

In June 2006, Jinsoo was one of 20 women owners of small businesses chosen for sponsorship by the Make Mine a Million $ Business (M3) program run by American Express, Cisco, and QVC. The following October she was approached by American Express to be featured as one of 10 small business owners from across the U.S. in its upcoming book celebrating its dedication to meeting the needs of small business owners, with a million copies to be published and distributed nationally.

Throughout her life and career, Jinsoo has shown a remarkable ability and tendency toward *winning,* despite the obstacles. She accomplishes everything she sets out to do through her positive attitude, persistence, and certainty that she can do it. And every day she works hard to give others the certainty that they too can do it.